MIND POWER
Into the 21st Century

Mind Power

Into the 21st Century

JOHN KEHOE

Published by Zoetic Inc.
6370 Chatham Street, West Vancouver, British Columbia
V7W 2E2, Canada
<http://www.kehoe-mindpower.com>

Distributed in U.S.A. by Associated Publishers Group
telephone 1-800-275-2606.

Canadian Cataloguing-in-Publication Data

Kehoe, John
      Mind power into the 21st century: techniques to
harness the astounding powers of thought

American ed.
ISBN 0-9697551-4-7

   1. Mental suggestion.   2. Thought and thinking.
3. Subconsciousness.   4. Mental healing.   5. Success.
I. Title.

BF637.S8K43 1997   158'.1   C97-900060-2

Printed in Canada by Best Gagne Book Manufacturers Inc.

John Kehoe

In 1975 John Kehoe withdrew into wooded seclusion to spend three years in intensive study and contemplation of the inner workings of the human mind. By borrowing freely from a wide variety of scientific and spiritual sources, and by applying his own shrewd observations and insights, Kehoe was able to forge the first straightforward and successful program for developing mind power. In 1978, he began teaching people the principles he had formulated, and by 1980 the phenomenal success of his speaking tours had grown to encompass the globe.

Kehoe has spent the last twenty years teaching, and he currently resides with his wife in the Pacific Northwest, from where he continues to write and tour.

Acknowledgments

To Joyce Hamilton, who helped me make the transition from speaking to writing and whose coaching helped make this book come alive. To Ric and Jennifer Beairsto for their suggestions and editing, to Soraya Othman, my business partner and friend, whose insistence that "the book get done!" propelled me into action, and finally to my wife, Sylvia, for her love, support and companionship. Thank you all.

John Kehoe

Contents

Preface

My goal in this book is to share with you a number of important techniques I have found useful in creating new realities. In *Mind Power Into the 21st Century* I will share with you stories of how people are successfully using these techniques and show you why they work so well.

Harnessing the forces of the universe and actively participating in the creative process of making your goals happen is an exhilarating experience. This book provides you with all the tools necessary to do that; all that remains is for you to apply them.

For twenty years I have had the joy and gratification of personally instructing well over one hundred thousand people in this system. Now, through this book, I will be able to reach countless others. If this book is in your hands for the first time, then welcome; I am sure you will benefit from what I've discovered, and I am very pleased to be able to introduce the Mind Power system to you.

John Kehoe

Another View of Reality

There are more things in heaven and earth than are dreamed of by mere mortal men.

—Shakespeare

To work with mind power you do not have to understand the laws of physics or how reality manifests itself, just as you don't have to understand how a carburetor works or how spark plugs fire in order to drive a car. Few of us understand automotive mechanics, but that doesn't stop us from driving. Likewise, in the science of mind power, anyone can quickly and successfully master the basics and effectively put them to work in his or her life.

We begin by examining the nature of reality, especially the startling new discoveries in science over the last twenty years which have helped us to understand more clearly how the mind creates its own reality. These discoveries explain why creating visualizations in our minds is not just idle daydreaming, but is a creative process which helps us control and direct the same energies that hold matter together, change water into steam, or cause a seed to sprout and grow.

Understanding the nature of these energies assists us in understanding the mind, and shows us why inspiration, prayer and intuition are not supernatural phenomenon at all, but follow patterns and laws which we can discover and use at our will. Like everything else in the known universe, the powers of the mind are governed by laws which, robbed of their scientific jargon and clearly presented, can be easily understood by anyone.

Let me take you on a short adventure into these new discoveries.

Modern physics now sees the universe as a vast, inseparable web of dynamic activity. Not only is the universe alive and constantly changing, but everything in the universe affects everything else. At its most primary level, the universe seems to be whole and undifferentiated, a fathomless sea of energy that permeates every object and every act. It is all one. In short, scientists are now confirming what mystics, seers and occultists have been telling us for thousands of years— we are not separate but part of one giant whole.

"When a blade of grass is cut, the whole universe quivers."
—ancient Upanishad saying

Modern physics has changed our concept of the material world. Particles are no longer seen as consisting of any basic "stuff"; rather they are seen as bundles of energy. They may make sudden transitions, "quantum leaps," behaving at times like units, yet on other occasions like waves of pure energy. Reality is fluid. Nothing is fixed. Everything is part of a pattern that is in constant motion; even a rock is a dance of energy. The universe is dynamic and alive and we are in it and of it, dynamic and alive ourselves.

THE UNIVERSE IS A GIANT HOLOGRAM

The theories that enabled the development of the hologram were first formulated in 1947 by Dennis Gabor, who later won a Nobel Prize for his discovery. A hologram is an entity in which "the whole" is contained in each and every one of its parts. For example, a starfish exhibits certain holographic patterns. If you cut a point from a starfish it will grow a new point. Not only that, the point will grow a whole new starfish, because the genetic imprint is contained in each and every one of its parts.

I was at a holographic exhibition several years ago in which I saw an exhibit of photographs done with holography. In one of the pictures was an image of a woman standing upright. If I moved to the right of the picture the woman changed suddenly and she was now smoking a cigarette; if I moved to the left of the picture it changed again and she had her hip thrown out in a suggestive pose. If one were to drop this holographic plate onto the floor and it shattered into pieces, each piece would reveal not what you would expect to see—a piece of her shoe or dress or maybe her eye—but the image of the whole woman. And if one moved any one of the little pieces from side to side, you would still see her smoke that cigarette and throw out her hip. Every single one of the small pieces would have the whole picture contained within it.

It now appears that the nature of reality is holographic,

and that the brain operates holographically as well. Our thinking processes seem to be identical to the primary state of the universe and made up of all the same "stuff." The brain is a hologram interpreting the holographic universe.

The main architects of this astounding idea were two of the world's most eminent thinkers: University of London physicist David Bohm, a protégé of Einstein's and one of the world's most respected quantum physicists, and Karl Pribram, a neurophysiologist at Stanford University. Coincidentally, they arrived at their findings independently of each other while working in totally separate fields of science. Bohm became convinced of the universe's holographic nature after years of frustration with the inability of more standard theories to explain all of the phenomena and results he was encountering in quantum physics. Pribram, in studying the human brain, also realized that standard theories' explanations of various neurophysiological puzzles simply didn't add up. For both men, the holographic model suddenly made sense and resolved a lot of unanswered questions. Both published their findings in the early 1970s. Their work received enormous response but unfortunately little of it was understood outside of the scientific community. While they had their detractors and skeptics (What new theory doesn't?), many of the world's most prominent physicists and scientists soon came on board. Cambridge's Brian Josephson, winner of the 1973 Nobel Prize in physics, described Bohm and Pribram's discoveries as involving "the most revolutionary breakthroughs in understanding the nature of reality." Dr. David Peat, a physicist at Queen's University in Canada and author of the book, *The Bridge Between Matter and Mind*, was another to agree: "Our thought processes are much more intimately connected to the physical world than any of us would suspect."

In 1979 at Princeton University, Robert G. Jahn, Dean of the School of Engineering and Applied Science, established a research program to explore the "role of consciousness in the establishment of physical reality." After thousands of controlled experiments, Jahn and his associates published their findings, stating that there was now sufficient evidence to indicate unequivocally that the mind can and does directly affect physical reality. By 1994 eminent scientists, educators and physicians from around the world were meeting at Princeton University to discuss how this startling new information might be extended and applied within their own fields and institutions.

All this is truly exciting news, and the implications are nothing less than staggering when one considers how we might use this new knowledge.

How consciousness and the physical world interact is now much less of a mystery: consciousness is but energy in its finest and most dynamic form. This helps explain why events are affected by what we imagine, visualize, desire, want or fear, and why and how an image held in the mind can be made real.

These discoveries about the nature of reality can be a major force for our continued change and growth. If we know and understand that we are a part of an open and dynamic universe, and that our minds play a decisive part in constructing reality, then we can choose to live more creatively and powerfully. We need no longer stand on the sidelines watching things happen to us, for with our new understanding we now realize that there are no sidelines to stand on, nor were there ever. Everything is affecting everything else. Wherever we go, whatever we do, our thoughts are creating our reality.

"Discovering a new theory," Einstein once said, "is like

climbing a mountain, gaining new and wider views." This is what you are doing by reading this book, and soon your mental climb will be rewarded by an open and exhilarating view of your true potential.

TWO

Consciousness

So think as if your every thought were to be etched in fire upon the sky for all and everything to see, for so, in truth, it is.

—Book of Mirdad

If you think of your thoughts as a reality existing side by side with what we call "the physical reality," you will be closer to understanding the unique relationship between the two.

You are living simultaneously in two worlds, two realities: the inner reality of your thoughts, emotions and attitudes, and the outer reality of people, places, things and events. Because we fail to separate these Inner and Outer worlds, we allow ourselves to become dominated by the Outer world of appearances, and we use the Inner world solely as a "mirror" for whatever happens to us. Our Inner world reacts constantly, and because we spend all of our time simply reacting, we never experience our power. Ironically, you begin changing your reality the day, the hour, the minute you cease *constantly* reacting to it.

Your inner consciousness is a powerful force whose influence is felt in every aspect of your life. It is, in fact, the major and most important part of who you are, and it is the main cause of your success or failure.

Everything at its purest and deepest essence is energy, and whenever you think, you are working with an immense amount of this energy in the quick, light, mobile form of thought. Thought is forever attempting to find form, is always looking for an outlet, is always trying to manifest itself. It is the nature of thought to try and materialize into its physical equivalent. Our normal thoughts can be compared to sparks from a fire. Though they contain the essence and potential power of the flame, they normally dissipate quickly. They last only a few seconds, fly into the air and quickly burn out.

Although a single unaided thought hasn't much power, through repetition the thought can become concentrated and directed, and its force can be magnified many times. The more the thought is repeated the more energy and power it generates, and the more readily it is able to manifest itself.

> *Weak and scattered thoughts are*
> *weak and scattered forces.*
> *Strong and concentrated thoughts are*
> *strong and concentrated forces.*

To illustrate this, picture a magnifying glass through which the sun's rays pass. If the magnifying glass is moved about from spot to spot, the power of the sun's rays is diffused and not apparent. If, however, the magnifying glass is held still and focused correctly at the proper height, those same rays become concentrated, and that diffused light suddenly becomes a force powerful enough to ignite a fire.

So it is with our thoughts. As you progress in your study of mind power you will learn how to develop and concentrate your thoughts so that they become much more powerful. At this point, just realize that thoughts have power in themselves. Your deeply held beliefs, your fears, your hopes, your worries, your attitudes, your desires, and each and every thought you think, all have an effect on you, others, and your environment.

Most of us go through our waking hours taking little notice of our thought processes: how the mind moves, what it fears, what it heeds, what it says to itself, what it brushes aside. For the most part we eat, work, converse, worry, hope, plan, make love, shop, play—all with minimal attention paid to *how* we think.

We might be far more willing to learn how to use our mental mechanisms if we imagined for a moment that for every thought we either gained a dollar or lost a dollar, depending on the type of thought. Considering we think thousands of thoughts every day, this is quite a proposition. Imagine an accounting system noting our every thought and recording which ones gained us money and which ones lost us money. How diligent we would be in controlling and directing our thoughts! How enthusiastically we would create those thoughts which made us money, and how carefully we would avoid those which cost us money.

This is, in fact, more or less what is already happening inside you, though with energy, not dollars. There *is* a big accounting system going on; it's called the universe, and no thought produced there is without its effect.

This world of ours is no dead pile of brick and stone. It is a living, vibrant system of energy. Every thought you think impresses itself upon this system, and its effect is indisputable. Whether you like it or not, you are forever creating your reality through what you are thinking.

The beginning step to a new and more successful life is absurdly easy. You have only to pay attention to the flow of thoughts inside your mind and direct it accordingly.

Your life is entirely of your own making, so look at the way you are living. You claim you want financial abundance, yet you are constantly bemoaning your lack of money and how expensive things are. You dwell on what you don't have and the bills coming in. You worry and wonder how you will get along. You may want financial abundance, but because your consciousness is of lack and worry, you will never experience that abundance.

Or maybe you wish you could find a new job, something interesting and challenging that would use your creativity and pay you well. If you constantly tell yourself these jobs are impossible to find, that it will never happen, it is very unlikely it ever *will* happen.

Perhaps you wish you could be a more outgoing individual, bold and spontaneous, full of assurance and confidence, yet if you constantly focus on your inferiorities and inadequacies and put yourself down, reminding yourself again and again of your problems, you are not likely to become that type of person. You may *want* strength, but if your consciousness is of weakness, you are fooling yourself to think you will ever possess that strength.

In short, *wanting something badly will not make it happen.* Hoping for something different will have no effect. Simply working hard, even if it's twelve to fifteen hours a day, is not enough. You will always remain where you are unless—and it's a big unless—*you change your thinking.*

> *"To them that hath . . . more shall be given. To them that hath not, even what little they have will be taken away."*
> —Luke 19:26

When I first read this quote I didn't think it was fair. It didn't seem fair that "them that had" would get more and "them that had not" would lose what little they had. It just didn't seem right. I thought it would be more just if "them that had not" were given more, but that is not what the Scripture says. This, according to the Bible, is not the way the universe works. But then, upon reflection, I realized that it was indeed fair. In fact what could be more fair than every person's freedom to choose for himself or herself thoughts which will, in turn, create their reality? There is great fairness in the complete freedom to determine the quality of one's life.

Want to change your circumstances? Develop the necessary consciousness. A successful person has a success consciousness. A wealthy person has developed a prosperity consciousness, and his thoughts are on abundance, success and prosperity. This is how *he* thinks.

"Easy for him," you say. "When you're successful it's easy to think success, and when you're wealthy it's easy to think prosperity, but my situation is totally different. I'm not successful; I'm not wealthy. The situations and circumstances of my life keep me down."

WRONG! Dead wrong! Your circumstances and situations never keep you down. The only things that keep you down and keep you stuck are your thoughts. With work and practice you can learn to direct your thoughts and create any consciousness you choose. Your reality will change only *after* you've developed your new consciousness, not before. *The new consciousness must come first.*

What is it that you want in your life? Do you know? More health? Then get health consciousness. More power? Then get power consciousness. More prosperity? Get prosperity consciousness. More happiness? Get happiness consciousness.

More spirituality? Get spiritual consciousness. Everything exists as a possibility. All that's required is for you to feed in the necessary energy until your objective becomes yours.

How reassuring it is to think that no matter what a person's past or present situation, no matter how many times he or she has previously failed, if that person would but regularly feed his or her consciousness, his or her situation would change! This remarkable ability has been given to each and every one of us to use or to ignore. It costs no money. It takes no special talent. It takes only the decision on your part to take the time and put forth the necessary effort to develop the appropriate consciousness. That's all! Everything else will automatically fall into place.

Your mind is like a garden which can be cultivated or neglected, and you are its master gardener. You can cultivate this garden, or you can ignore it and let it develop whatever way it will. But make no mistake: you will reap the harvest of your work or your neglect!

> *Your mind creates your reality.*
> *You can choose to accept this or not.*
> *You can be conscious of it and set*
> *your mind working for you, or you*
> *can ignore it and allow it to work*
> *in ways that will hinder and hold*
> *you back. But your mind will always*
> *and forever be creating your reality.*

THREE

Visualization

*There is no thought in my mind
but it quickly tends to convert
itself into a power and organizes
a huge instrumentality of means.*
—Ralph Waldo Emerson

What is it that makes a person a winner? What distinguishes those who succeed from those who fail?

"It's all in the mind," says Arnold Schwarzenegger. A multimillionaire, successful real estate tycoon, movie star, body-builder, five-time winner of the Mr. Universe title, Arnold has it made. But it wasn't always so. Arnold can remember back when he had nothing except a belief that his mind was the key to getting where he wanted to go.

"When I was very young, I visualized myself being and having what it was I wanted. Mentally I never had any doubts about it. The mind is really so incredible. Before I won my first Mr. Universe, I walked around the tournament like I owned it. The title was already mine. I had won it so many times in my mind that there was no doubt I would win it. Then when I moved on to the movies, the same thing. I visualized myself being a successful actor and earning big money. I could feel and taste success. I just knew it would all happen."

Chris Poellein was a member of the world-renowned West German freestyle ski team that won the European Cup six times between 1976 and 1982.

"Part of our training program involved working with a psychologist to increase the power of our minds. After training on the slopes we were placed in a state of meditation and encouraged to totally repeat the slope runs in our minds, visualizing each bump and movement of the routine. We worked as hard training mentally as we did physically. Excellence in athletics—or indeed any endeavor—depends primarily on having a clear mental picture of that activity."

Chris should know; she not only has her six medals, but she now has her own successful consulting firm working with business and sports groups to show them how they, too, can benefit from the same techniques.

Bryan Edwards, a man of infectious good humor and high spirits, sells life insurance. I met him on one of my tours and he has become a good friend. Each evening, before he goes to bed, he spends ten minutes running over in his mind his next day's calls. He pictures himself making his presentation to each client. He sees them being receptive and gladly taking out a policy with him. He imagines a very productive day with lots of sales. He does this for ten minutes before he goes to bed and ten minutes upon rising in the morning, a total of twenty minutes each day. Bryan Edwards sells more insurance in one week than most people sell in six months, and is consistently in the top one percent of his profession every year.

Three totally different people with totally different goals

and objectives in life, yet all are using the same technique to create and influence their reality—the technique of visualization.

Visualization is using your imagination to see yourself in a situation that hasn't yet happened, picturing yourself having or doing the thing you want, and successfully achieving the results you desire.

For example, let us say you want to be more confident. Using visualization you picture yourself as confident. You see yourself doing things, talking to people, all with great confidence. You picture yourself in situations that normally give you difficulty and you see yourself in these situations at ease, confident, and performing well. You might picture your friends and associates complimenting you, congratulating you on your new-found confidence. You feel the pride and satisfaction of both being a confident person and of enjoying the things that happen to you as a result of your confidence. You visualize everything that would or could happen to you and live as if it really *is* happening to you.

HERE'S HOW TO GO ABOUT
A SUCCESSFUL VISUALIZATION

1. Decide what you want to do: pass an exam, gain a promotion, meet someone new, make lots of money, be more confident, win the squash game.
2. Relax. Spend several minutes unwinding so that you are comfortable in body and mind.
3. Spend five to ten minutes visualizing the reality you want.

Linger on thoughts of doing and having the thing you want, not as some future reality that *might* happen or *could* happen. Live in your mind as if it's happening to you right now. Create little inner film clips or videos. See yourself doing the thing you want. On one level, you know it's not yet happening to you; it's not yet real. It's still just a visualization, a mental picture. But the mental pictures we indulge in, the ones we regularly think about, become a blueprint for our goals, a mold into which we pour our energy. These pictures are real forces that will work for us.

Build whatever characteristics are necessary in your visualization. If talent, courage, determination or persistence are vital parts of the picture, include them. Sometimes you will see clear, sharp images, as if you are watching yourself featured in a movie, accomplishing your goal. Other times, you just sort of "think about" your goals in a general way; this is all fine. You can alternate between precise and free-flowing visualization, doing a few minutes of each, or concentrate on whatever technique feels most comfortable.

Precise Visualization: Generate the exact pictures and scenes you want in your mind. Follow the preset script you have created and run it through your mind a number of times.

Free-Flowing Visualization: Allow images and thoughts to come and go without choosing them directly, *as long as they show a positive outcome of your goal*.

Practice both methods and remember the key here is *practice*. Most people find that they have difficulty in the beginning stages of visualization. Their minds won't cooperate and picture the desired scenes. Don't worry if this happens; the picture doesn't have to be complete and perfect. If you commit yourself to a program of regular visualization, you will be surprised at how your mind will gradually begin to think the thoughts and create the scenes you choose for it.

I should mention at this point that visualizing something

once or twice is of little effect. Results come when the image is imprinted again and again and *again* for a period of weeks or months until your goal has been achieved. Don't try to measure success after only one or two attempts.

If doubts or contradictory thoughts arise, and occasionally they will, just ignore them. Don't try to resist them or fight them, simply let those thoughts come and go in your consciousness without much notice. Just keep repeating your visualization and everything will quite naturally look after itself.

TWO CONDITIONS FOR A SUCCESSFUL VISUALIZATION

1. Always visualize your goal as if it's actually happening to you right now. Make it real in your mind; make it detailed. Enter the role and become it in your mind.
2. Visualize your goal at least once a day, each and every day. There is power in repetition.

Any thought put into your mind, and nourished regularly, will produce results in your life.

Let me share with you a now famous and well-documented experiment conducted by psychologist Alan Richardson. A group of student basketball players was divided into three groups, tested for their ability to score baskets, and each group's results were recorded. The first group was then directed to come into the gym every day for a month to practice shooting, the second group was instructed to engage in no practice at all, and the third group was instructed to engage in a very different sort of practice. They didn't step foot in the gym, but instead stayed in their dorms mentally imagining themselves there practicing. For half an hour each day they "saw" themselves shooting and scoring and improving dramatically. They continued this inner "practice" every day. After a month, the three groups were tested again.

The first group (those who practiced shooting every day) showed a 24 percent improvement in their scores. The second group (those who did no practice) showed no improvement. And the third group—who, remember, had practiced only in their minds—improved equally as much as the group that had practiced for real!

Such creative visualization is powerful, but it's far from magic. It involves working with natural laws and energies and being creative in directing your own innate power.

Properly directed, your imagination is one of the most dynamic faculties that you possess. Begin using this technique right away. You don't need to concern yourself with the specifics of how things will unfold. Trust the process. Supply follows demand, and you will be led to do the right thing at the right time. You can be sure that the ways and means will make themselves known to you, for nature always creates the opportunities needed to fulfill the demands put upon her.

It's natural to want all the answers before we're willing to risk any legwork. We'd all love to see the steps and know all the details of everything that will happen to us. But you rarely get to see those details and steps at the beginning, and very often things unfold in the most unexpected ways.

Actress Carol Burnett was born in Los Angeles and raised by her grandmother. They scraped by on welfare and were so poor that her grandmother collected toilet paper from public washrooms. There certainly was not enough money to send the talented youngster to UCLA, which was Carol's dream. She, however, knew that one day she was going to attend the university. "I never thought about the possibility of not going. I would imagine myself taking the classes, being on the campus, learning everything I wanted to learn. Every day I would think about it. Even though there didn't seem to be any way I could go, I knew I would."

So how did she get the money?

"One day in my final year of high school I went to the mailbox to check the mail. There was an envelope made out to me. It had a stamp on it, but it wasn't postmarked. It hadn't been mailed, it had been hand-delivered by someone. I opened the envelope and in it was the exact amount of my first year's tuition. No note. No explanation. Just the money. I still, to this day, don't know who sent it."

OPPORTUNITIES OPEN UP WHEN
YOU OPEN UP YOUR THOUGHTS!

Now I am not saying that if you visualize it, someone will come up with an envelope and give you the exact money you want, the way it happened for Carol Burnett. But I do promise you that situations and opportunities will come your way that will lead you to your goal—you can count on it. Your thoughts are more powerful than you suspect, and any image held in the mind is a force that will eventually produce an effect.

It is not futuristic science fiction that we possess this ability; it already exists within us as a practical tool which we can use any time we choose.

FOUR
Seeding

When an object or purpose is clearly held in thought, its precipitation, in tangible and visible form, is merely a question of time. The vision always precedes the realization.

—Lillian Whiting

If visualization is creating scenes or pictures in your own movie, then seeding is like adding the sound track, only instead of words you are adding the *feelings* that accompany the pictures. For example, let's say you have an important presentation to make to your company. Your supervisors and bosses will all be present. If you do well there is an excellent chance you'll be promoted as a result. The presentation is very important to your career. You decide to use the seeding technique, spending five to ten minutes seeding the thought and feeling that you've just given the presentation and it was a huge success. Everyone was impressed. The interview is all over and you did it—you pulled off a fabulous presentation!

Unlike visualization, in seeding you are primarily concerned with the *feeling* of whatever it is you are visualizing. Here is where your imagination comes into play. Imagine what it would be like to have delivered the "perfect" presentation. Would you be excited, elated, overjoyed, relieved, thrilled? Whatever your personal reaction, feel it in your guts and make those physical feelings a part of you. Live in the certainty that you already have the thing that you want. Don't wish, wonder, worry, or hope that it will go well. Claim it in your mind as an already existing fact. Replace "It's going to go well," with "It has gone well." It's all over and you did it, so enjoy the feeling of excitement, the sense of accomplishment, and the thrill of pulling it off! Congratulate yourself. Shout for joy. Leap up and down if you like. Exalt and vibrate again and again with the feeling of having already accomplished your goal.

Again, in seeding, you are not primarily interested in the mental pictures of how you'll achieve your goal, though these pictures will quite naturally flow into your mind; rather it is the physical sensation of accomplishment you're after: the flushed cheeks, the pounding heart, the sweaty palms.

In the Bible, Jesus' disciples ask him to teach them how to pray. (You may or may not believe in the teachings of the Bible. It does, however, contain some very powerful insights into mind power techniques.) Jesus replies, "Whatever things ye pray for and ask for believing that ye have received, ye shall receive them." Notice he says that you must believe you *have* received them—not that you *will* receive them, but that you *have* received them—therefore you *will* receive them. This is more than just hoping or wishing, this is claiming what you want in the inner world, the world of thought and creative energy, and is a very powerful process, as any person adept in applying mind power will attest.

Let me share with you a story that happened to two very good friends of mine, Bill and Janet Henderson. The Hendersons were moving to a major city from a rural area, and they wanted to buy a house roomy enough to accommodate their growing family. Of course, houses are much more expensive in the city, and they were a large family needing a large house. They also had very specific needs; not only did they want a large house, they wanted a large yard with lots of trees, and all at a price within their budget. Everyone told them they would never find anything like that for the price they wanted to pay, but they knew better. Bill had already practiced mind power techniques both in his job and in his relationship with his family, and knew they worked, so he enlisted Janet and together they worked as a team, visualizing and seeding for the house.

Two months later, they called me and asked me to come see their new home. We walked around their spacious yard, as tranquil with its trees, shrubs and flowers as if they had taken a piece of the country and brought it with them. Once inside, they gave me the full tour. It was a spacious house with enough bedrooms to give all the children their own rooms, and there was a den and a recreation room—all for the price they had wanted to pay!

"That's fabulous!" I said, "Aren't you surprised you found it?"

Bill's answer showed such an enlightened understanding of the powers of the mind that I've never forgotten it. "No," he said. "We're not surprised at all. In our minds we had already taken possession of the house two months ago."

He said it with such confidence. After all, this was only the manifestation of something he had been claiming as his for two months. Bill and Janet had claimed the house in their inner world; they had taken possession of it already. Those are strong words. Strong vibrations. Powerful faith. They weren't hoping or wishing or wondering when and where they would find their dream house. They just worked regularly with the "feeling" that a house which would meet their needs would be theirs. They "took possession of it in their minds." Not this specific house, for until it came their way they had no idea it even existed. But they did know what they wanted and needed, and this is what they seeded every day until it became their reality.

Today the Hendersons not only use seeding and other mind power techniques in their own lives, they are teaching their children the same principles so they, too, can have rich and rewarding lives. What greater gift could a parent give to their children than an understanding of their own natural powers?

We all have this power. Our thoughts create our reality, and seeding is merely working with the thought that you already have the thing you want.

Once again it is repetition and consistency that separate seeding from idle daydreaming. In seeding, you don't live an illusion. You don't walk around every day with your head in the clouds literally believing you possess something you don't. Seeding is a mind power exercise that takes five minutes a day, a five-minute burst of energy that you create for yourself regularly, each and every day, without fail. The importance of repetition cannot be overemphasized. As with all mind power techniques, practicing sporadically here and there will have little effect. Set yourself up a regular program and keep to it. Regularly seed the feeling that you already have whatever it is you want. It's yours. Live it. Vibrate with it. Exalt and thrill with it. Claim it, absolutely, as yours. Take possession of it in the inner world.

TWO CONDITIONS FOR SUCCESSFUL SEEDING

1. Always seed with the feeling that you have the thing you want, that you have already achieved it.
2. Seed regularly, each and every day, for at least five minutes. It is infinitely better to practice a few minutes every day than to do it for an hour once a week.

Affirmations

*The possibilities of thought training
are infinite, its consequences
eternal, and yet few take the pains
to direct their thinking into
channels that will do them good,
but instead leave all to chance.*
                        —Brice Marden

Affirmations are probably the easiest and simplest technique I know of to influence and affect the conscious mind. They have been used for centuries throughout the world in such spiritual and magical practices as prayers and mantras. Now they are being used by people from all walks of life to close business deals, heal ailments, meet people, win tournaments, and in countless other applications.

Affirmations are simple statements repeated to yourself silently or aloud, whatever feels most comfortable and practical to you at the time. You can do them anywhere—in your car while you're driving, sitting in a doctor's office waiting for an appointment, lying in bed before you go to sleep. You decide upon a statement that represents what you want to have happen to you, and you repeat it to yourself over and over again.

For example, let's say you're in a situation that usually upsets you and makes you tense when you'd prefer to be relaxed and calm. This is the perfect time to use an affirmation. Quietly repeat to yourself, "I feel calm and relaxed. I feel calm and relaxed. I feel calm and relaxed." Don't try forcing yourself to *feel* calm and relaxed, just keep repeating the statement to yourself for a couple of minutes. Likewise, if you have a big meeting coming up and you want it to go well, begin affirming to yourself beforehand, "It's going to be a great meeting. It's going to be a great meeting. It's going to be a great meeting."

WHAT ARE YOU DOING
WHEN YOU DO AFFIRMATIONS?

When you are doing affirmations you are influencing the thoughts that occur in your mind. Your mind can hold only one thought at a time, so an affirmation works by "filling" your mind with thoughts that support your goal. The words suggest to the mind what it should be thinking. If you're affirming to yourself, "It's going to be a great meeting," your mind will quite naturally begin thinking related thoughts about it being a great meeting. Your mind effortlessly picks up the implications and message of your affirmation. It sounds very simple, but this technique can be remarkably effective in helping you gain the results you want.

Make whatever you want to see happen into an appropriate affirmation and use it regularly. One successful salesman I know begins each day with the affirmation, "Lots of sales, lots of smiles," and he repeats this to himself for several minutes in the morning and several times throughout the day.

THINGS TO REMEMBER WHEN
YOU ARE DOING AFFIRMATIONS

1. You don't necessarily have to believe them! In fact, anyone who's ever been unsuccessful in using affirmations has probably been trying to force themselves to do just that. This mistake can actually nullify the effects of the affirmation. Don't worry about believing, just keep repeating. If you do believe what you are affirming, great! If you don't believe it, that's fine too. It doesn't matter. The conscious mind will quite naturally pick up the content of whatever you are affirming, and the correct thoughts will seep into your consciousness. You don't have to force anything.

2. Always affirm in the positive. Make a positive statement, not a negative one. For example, if you want to see a meeting go well, you wouldn't say, "I'm not going to blow this meeting." If you want to be calm and relaxed you wouldn't affirm, "I'm not going to be uptight." For some reason the mind doesn't pick up the "not" and you find yourself programming "blow the meeting" or "uptight." The mind will focus on these self-destructive images and not on what you want.

3. Keep your affirmation short. An affirmation should be like a mantra: short and simple, easy to say, and easy to repeat. I like to keep my affirmations to ten words or less. Sometimes even two words can be very effective: "tremendous success" or "record sales."

I have had people show me affirmations that were half a page long. There's no way you can say an affirmation that long repeatedly. Even two sentences is too long. Repetition is what will imprint your affirmation into your consciousness, so the shorter the better. I repeat: make it short, make it rhythmic, make it easy to say.

Be careful that you don't use affirmations against yourself without realizing it.

"I'll never get it done,"

"I'll never do it,"

"It's impossible,"

"I'm blowing it,"

"I'm a disaster at relationships,"

"I know I'm going to make a mistake,"

"I'm always losing,"

are all affirmations that you can find yourself repeating to yourself without even realizing it. Watch out for them.

Let me share with you an experience that happened to me on a recent lecture tour. Halfway through the tour, I looked at my schedule for the following months and couldn't believe my eyes. I was being routed from one city to another with hardly any breaks and was even expected to be in two different cities on the same day! I began thinking that the upcoming month would be an impossible, stress-filled pressure cooker, and that's what I actually started telling myself—"This is going to be a pressure cooker." For two or three days I felt increasingly tense and uptight in anticipation of the dreadful next leg of the tour. I cursed the person who had set this ridiculous schedule for me.

Then I caught myself. I had to laugh. Here I was teaching mind power, and I'd unwittingly fallen into a trap of my own making. Nice affirmation, "I'm in a pressure cooker!" So I made myself a new affirmation focusing on just three words:

Organized, Relaxed, and *Fun,* and I repeated this to myself for several minutes. The next morning I began the day with the same affirmation, and I repeated it whenever I started thinking about my hectic schedule. Within a few days I began thinking that as long as I was organized and relaxed, the marathon pace might be fun. What was I getting all upset about?

In the end, those three words made all the difference. My schedule didn't change, but my attitude towards it did. The tour that I had almost made into a pressure cooker for myself turned out to be a breeze. I was organized, relaxed, and had fun rushing about to meet the challenge, once I changed from a negative to a positive affirmation.

You too can create affirmations and use them throughout your day to help you accomplish the things you want. They are easy to say and can be done anywhere—in the bank line-up, in the waiting room, or when stuck in traffic. You don't have to believe them. You don't have to do them with the literal belief that you "have it." All you have to do is repeat them! I'd suggest starting first thing in the morning, because that crucial first half-hour sets the tone for the rest of your day. As little as two or three minutes of practice will soon produce a noticeable effect.

"Every day in every way, it's getting better and better."

The name Emile Coué may not be commonly known today, but at the turn of the century, this pioneer in affirmation techniques was curing illnesses and teaching his discoveries in clinics all over Europe and North America. He caused quite a sensation in his day and his work is still talked about today, decades after his death. Coué found that his patients recovered much better, and more quickly, if they repeated a simple affirmation every morning upon rising, and every evening before going to sleep. The affirmation he taught them was, "Every day in every way I'm getting better and better." Two minutes in the morning. Two minutes in the evening. That's all. The effect was so dramatic that he wrote several books on the subject of self-suggestion and taught people around the world the curative properties of the mind when directed towards recovery. Coué's affirmation focused the patient's mind on every day, in every way, getting better and better. Emile Coué is credited with the documented cures of thousands of people.

Closer to our own time, singer-songwriter John Lennon will always be remembered for his music, his humanitarian beliefs, and his wonderful openness. Lennon made no secret of his interest in magic and the powers of the mind, and his songs reflect this interest. Listen to his lyrics for the song, "Mind Games":

> We're playing our mind games . . .
> Creating the future, out of the now . . .

Lennon knew and used both visualization and affirmations. "My mind is what makes it all happen," he liked to say, and in "Beautiful Boy," which he wrote for his son, Sean, he actually sings, "Before you go to sleep—say this little prayer—Every day in every way, it's getting better and better." He, like Coué and so many other great men and women before him, found his way to this eternal truth.

John Lennon's songs beckoned us to believe in ourselves and to believe in our power and our ability. "Who do you think you are?" he sang, "A superstar? Well, right you are!"

Acknowledging

Nothing succeeds like success.

Most of us are quicker to see our own failures and shortcomings than we are to acknowledge our achievements and successes. When we accomplish something we feel good about it for a few days or weeks, but then we move on to new goals and new desires. All too quickly we leave behind the good feelings of accomplishment; we forget that we have even achieved those things. Our new desires and wants become our focus and we let go of the success vibration that was created from our past achievements. This is a complete waste of powerful success energy. If we focus only on the not yet attained, we unconsciously feed the mind the idea that we are lacking. We can reuse success energies from past achievements again and again, with very positive results, but unfortunately, we rarely do so.

One night after one of my lectures, a woman approached me and asked, "John, do you think I could ever achieve my goals?" I asked her to describe them. Her first goal was to live in a beautiful house, her second goal was to fly back to England to see parents and relatives she hadn't seen in fourteen years, and her third goal was to have a meaningful relationship with someone special. As she was a single mother with three children and lived on very slender means, these goals seemed impossible to her at the time. From my seminars, however, she hoped to learn powerful new ways to create a better reality.

I assured her that, by using mind powers, she could indeed achieve her goals, and didn't really think of the woman again until about a year later when I received a phone call from her. "John," she said excitedly, "you'll never guess what happened! I now live in a new house with a swimming pool and a fabulous yard and view." I told her I was very happy for her, but she wasn't finished. "Not only that, but I was in England for three weeks and saw my family. And . . . ," you could tell she was leaving the best for last, "I'm in the most fabulous relationship. I'm in love, really in love!"

Needless to say, I looked forward to seeing her again. Months passed before I did, but she met me at the airport, and the first thing I noticed about her was that she didn't appear to be the bright, exuberant woman I was expecting to see. When she said to me, rather despondently, "John, why doesn't mind power work for me?" I could only look at her incredulously.

"Why doesn't mind power work for me?" she repeated. I couldn't believe I was hearing this. I said, "Listen, correct me if I'm wrong, but aren't you the woman who one year ago wanted to live in a nice house, travel to England, and have a meaningful relationship? Wasn't that you?"

She looked at me in embarrassment. "Oh," she said "I forgot about that!"

Forgot about that! How could anyone forget about it?

Well, it's easy. We do it all the time. She had achieved her previous goals and now was working on new and different ones. Because she hadn't yet realized her new goals she was sincerely wondering why mind power wasn't working for her. She had totally forgotten and taken for granted her most recent achievements. Her mind had moved on to new things.

We focus on what we want to achieve, totally forgetting to acknowledge what we *have* achieved. Why concern yourself with what you're not? We all have areas where we've failed, where we feel we don't measure up. Learn to pat yourself on the back for your present or past victories, no matter how small. Look for anything that makes you feel strong, victorious, successful and good about yourself. Acknowledge anything and everything, small and large, and use it to create a vibration of success and achievement "in the now" which will aid you in attracting further success.

Acknowledgment is especially effective when you are trying to achieve new goals. For example, let's say you're a young filmmaker trying to break into the big time by getting a major production company to back you. Using the acknowledging technique, you could look for areas that make you feel confident in your capabilities as a filmmaker. You might focus your thoughts on some of the short films you've made in the past and are proud of. You might recall certain scenes that the critics said either worked well or showed real promise. Focus on these scenes and remind yourself that you also have a good eye for detail. Acknowledge all the hard work you've put into learning your craft. Recall all the compliments and praise people have given you about your work, and recognize all the skills you've developed over the last few years and the progress you've made.

Search, and I emphasize the word "search," for things to acknowledge. Don't just acknowledge the obvious; acknowledge everything. Don't feel silly or think it doesn't matter.

Your positive qualities are just as real as the negative ones. Go ahead and feel proud. Feel great. Feel successful. Let your mind linger for several minutes on the success you already are.

This technique can be applied to any goal, not just in specific areas, but in a general way as well. Take ten minutes out right now and write down every strong point you can come up with in any area of your life, past or present.

Examples:

> I dress well.
> I'm good at my job.
> I'm very creative.
> I know a lot about _____.
> I'm a good conversationalist.
> I'm generous.
> I'm a good painter.
> I have a positive attitude.
> I'm a safe driver.
> I'm fun to be with.

Don't stop now. Your positive qualities are endless!

> People like me.
> I work hard.
> I enjoy life.
> I'm a loving partner.
> I'm a conscientious parent.
> I support my family and friends.
> I've just completed making my acknowledging list.

Make a general list and make it *long*. List at least twenty items. Don't be timid and reserved about it—put it all down in black and white so you can see, in a concrete way, how many reasons you have to feel good about yourself. That's the purpose of this exercise, to make you realize you have lots of reasons to be proud of yourself. These good feelings create the success vibration that will form the foundation of your future success.

You can employ a similar approach when you are attempting to achieve any goal. Make a list of at least ten things about yourself which you can acknowledge that will support you in your attempt to achieve that goal. In trying to get a job as a sales manager, for example, you could make a list acknowledging the qualities that would make you a success at the job and, thus, the best candidate for the position.

Your list might look something like this:

> I'm great with people.
> I'm a good communicator.
> People like me.
> I work well with people.
> I'm a born salesman.
> I've done well in all my previous jobs.
> I can motivate people.
> I'm talented.
> I look and dress well.
> I'm organized.
> I work hard.
> I achieve my goals.

If you hadn't made your list, you might have gone into the interview just *hoping* they'd give you the job. This way you go in certain that you are qualified for the job.

"Nothing succeeds like success," and you *have* already succeeded in numerous areas. The more you vibrate this energy, the more success you attract from the environment. So make your lists. Feed your mind. Work with energy. Get involved in your life. Never stop acknowledging yourself. Never stop believing in yourself. Don't wait for things to happen—begin creating, as John Lennon said, "the future out of the now."

Acknowledge. Acknowledge. Acknowledge.

CONSCIOUSNESS CREATES REALITY
AND
YOU CREATE CONSCIOUSNESS

SEVEN

The Subconscious Mind

*The power to move the world is in
your subconscious mind.*

—William James

We possess within us two minds. So far I have written only of the conscious mind. I would now like to introduce you to your second mind, the hidden and mysterious subconscious. Our subconscious mind contains such power and complexity that it literally staggers the imagination. We know that this subconscious mind controls and orchestrates our bodily functions, from pumping blood to all parts of our body to regulating our breathing and digestion. We further know that the subconscious has recorded every event that has ever happened to us. Every incident in our personal history is recorded within, along with the emotions and thoughts evoked by those incidents.

It is also from this second mind that we can receive invaluable guidance and direction. Through our intuition, dreams, feelings and hunches, our subconscious will bring to us the ideas, insights and solutions needed to satisfy all our needs and desires. We are never alone or without guidance once we have awakened this inner faculty.

And finally the subconscious is the mechanism through which thought impulses which are repeated regularly with feeling and emotion are quickened, charged and changed into their physical equivalent. You may voluntarily plant in your subconscious mind any plan, thought or purpose which you desire to translate into its physical counterpart, and that counterpart will manifest itself for you. The subconscious is creative, prolific and ever-ready to serve you. Yet so few of us understand how to use its power.

In order to understand how the conscious and subconscious minds work together as a team to create your reality, let me again use an analogy. Your subconscious mind is like fertile soil which accepts any seed you plant within it. Your habitual thoughts and beliefs are the seeds which are being constantly sown within, and they produce in your life what is planted just as surely as corn kernels produce corn. You will reap what you sow. This is a law.

Remember, the conscious mind is the gardener. It is our responsibility to be aware of and choose wisely what reaches the inner garden. But unfortunately for most of us our role as gardener has never been explained to us. And in misunderstanding our role, we have allowed seeds of all types, both good and bad, to enter our inner garden. This then is the cause of all that is happening in our life. If you wish to understand why fortune or misfortune is happening to you in any area of your life, you need only look within.

The subconscious will not discriminate. It will manifest failure, ill health and misfortune just as easily as success and abundance. It works to reproduce in our life according to what seeds we have nurtured within. Your subconscious accepts what is impressed upon it with feeling and emotion whether these thoughts are positive or negative. It does not evaluate things like your conscious mind, and it does not argue with you.

If you want to make changes in your life, you must look to the cause, and the cause is the way you are using the conscious mind—the way you are thinking and picturing in your mind. You cannot think both negative and positive thoughts at the same time. One or the other must dominate. The mind is a creature of habit, so it becomes your responsibility to make sure that positive emotions and thoughts constitute the dominating influence of your mind.

In order to change external conditions, you must first change the internal. Most people try to change conditions and circumstances by working directly with those conditions and circumstances. This always proves futile, or at the very best temporary, unless it is accompanied by a change of thoughts and beliefs.

Awakening to this truth, the way to a better, more successful life becomes crystal clear. Train your conscious mind to think thoughts of success, happiness, health, prosperity, and to weed out fear and worry. Keep your conscious mind busy with the expectation of the best, and make sure the thoughts you habitually think are based upon what you want to see happen in your life.

Here the "law of habit" can assist you. Form the habit of practicing daily all the principles contained in this book. Don't just read the chapters, but take the principles and techniques into your life and make them a living reality for you.

Water takes the shape of whatever container holds it, whether it be in a glass, a vase or a river bank. Likewise, your subconscious will create and manifest according to the images you habitually project upon it through your daily thinking. This is how your destiny is created. Your life is in your hands, to make of it what you choose.

SYNCHRONICITY

Once you grasp that your subconscious will bring to you whatever you need, and you begin working daily projecting the thoughts and images of what you want, seemingly chance and fortuitous events will begin to happen to you. Your powerful inner collaborator, working with your instructions, will bring to you the people and circumstances you require to fulfill your goals. "A thousand unseen hands," as Joseph Campbell describes them, will come to your aid. Synchronicity appears to the uninitiated to be coincidence or luck, but it is neither. It is simply the operation of natural laws which you have set in motion with your thoughts.

Let me explain how it works. I wrote earlier of all physical reality consisting of particles of energy. We live in a giant web of energy. When, for example, you begin imprinting success upon your subconscious mind, it sets up a continuous vibration of this energy that resonates upon the whole. The subconscious works day and night with this success vibration, attracting to you the people and circumstances necessary for your success. I might also add that the subconscious will work equally hard to attract to you the circumstances necessary for your failure if that is how you habitually think. It does not discriminate or censor, but works with the thoughts, desires, hopes and fears that you allow to dwell in your conscious mind.

We are fortunate that the laws of physical reality and the laws of the mind are now beginning to be understood. In years past, it might have seemed incredible that we could at-tract and create our reality through this process, yet now, with these new insights, we know how it works. Our thoughts being energy, it only makes sense that our repeated images, affirmations, visualizations, deeply held beliefs, fears and de-sires, vibrating within the larger web of reality, would have an affect upon that reality. In fact, when you stop and really think about it, since we are all connected, how could it be otherwise?

Let me repeat once again this all-important point. When you unite mentally and emotionally with the good you wish to embody, the creative powers of your subconscious will re-spond accordingly. Your habitual thinking and imagery mold your reality and create your ultimate destiny.

The Universe is prodigal in its support of us. We unfortu-nately are miserly in what we accept. But this can change. Once you understand the laws of your life and begin seeing how they can work for you, you will eagerly embrace them. Begin this very day to imprint upon your subconscious what it is you desire. Let nothing deter you from this practice, and then watch with wonder and excitement as the synchronicity doors begin opening. In the words of Himalayan explorer W. H. Murray, "The moment one definitely commits oneself then Providence moves too. All sorts of things occur to help one that would otherwise never have occurred. A whole stream of events issue from the decision, raising in one's favor all manner of incidents and meetings and material assistance which no man would have believed would have come his way."

Know this truth and you will possess a key to the treasures of the Universe. The power of your subconscious is awaiting your instructions.

Intuition

Why do I always get my best ideas in the shower?

—Albert Einstein

Imagine how confident, enthusiastic and secure you would feel if you could team up with a partner who was able to supply you with everything you need in life. A partner who would give you solutions to your problems, show you exciting new opportunities and how to take advantage of them, and be there for you with wise and reliable advice whenever you needed it. Well, you do indeed possess such a partner—the partner within, your intuition.

All great achievers, whether they be businessmen, athletes, artists or statesmen, trust and use their intuition. The ability to come up with inspired ideas and make astute decisions is one of the primary secrets of success, and the mark of one who has cultivated his inner self.

I once had a chance meeting with one of Australia's richest and boldest entrepreneurs. We were in a hotel lobby one evening about an hour before I was due to speak. I recognized him from his pictures in various newspapers and magazines, so I approached him and introduced myself. I had read in a magazine article that he believed strongly in intuition and I asked him if that was true. "Intuition plays a major role in everything I do," he confirmed. "I can't think of one major venture that I have entered upon without first checking with my intuition."

This man is not alone. Mozart claimed he received his inspiration from within. Socrates said he was guided by his inner voice. Einstein, Edison, Marconi, Henry Ford, Luther Burbank, Madame Curie, Nobel laureates by the bundle, the list goes on and on of great men and women who have attributed their success directly to their intuition.

Henry Mintzberg, in the *Harvard Business Review*, describes a study he conducted on high-ranking corporate executives in which he found that they were "constantly relying on hunches to cope with problems too complex for rational thinking." He concluded: "Success does not lie in that narrow-minded concept called 'rationality'; it lies in a blend of clear-headed logic and powerful intuition." Billionaire Ted Turner, founder of CNN and currently one of the richest men in the world, shares similar sentiments: "Vision and intuition go hand in hand with one another."

Conrad Hilton tells the story of how he submitted a bid of $165,000 for a piece of property he wished to purchase for a hotel. When he awoke the following morning the number 180,000 was nagging him. "Connie" was well known for following his hunches, so he changed his bid to $180,000. He secured the property, which eventually sold for over $2 million, because the next highest bid was $179,000.

Ray Kroc bought McDonald's against the advice of his lawyers and accountants because, "I felt it in my funny bone that it was a sure thing." McDonald's is now a very sure thing; it's the most successful franchise operation in the world, and

Kroc's decision to buy "a few hamburger" stands made him a multimillionaire hundreds of times over.

Paying attention to intuition enables an individual to make better decisions, to come up with more creative ideas and deeper insights, and to find the smoothest, most direct route from desire to fulfillment. Those people who always seem to be in the right place at the right time, and for whom good things happen with uncanny frequency, are not just lucky; they have developed an intuitive sense of what to do and when to do it. Their intuition allows them to go beyond the obvious to come up with fresh, innovative possibilities. It supplies them with all they need to know, and instructs them on when and how to use that knowledge.

Cognitive scientists who study how information flows through the brain tell us that only a small fraction of what the mind takes in, less than one percent, ever reaches conscious awareness. It is staggering to think of how much we're missing. Yet this information is available to you. I wrote earlier of our minds as being bits of a greater hologram, with the whole contained in each and every one of its parts. Your everyday conscious mind may know and understand only your own personal experiences and knowledge, but your subconscious mind is linked and connected to the entire system, and thus has access to all the information contained within that system. Your intuition is how you access it.

GETTING ANSWERS

Preparation

Immerse yourself with all the available facts and information. Give the subconscious as much material to work with as possible. Search out any and all knowledge that is relevant. Open yourself to anything that is even vaguely relevant to what you're working on. The idea is to gather such a broad and varied range of data that unusual and unlikely elements can begin to juxtapose themselves. Let your imagination roam freely. Immerse yourself in this information without necessarily trying to make sense of it; this is the job of the subconscious.

Incubation

Once you have mulled over all the relevant pieces, you can let the problem simmer. Whereas preparation demands active work, incubation is more passive. Let go and let the subconscious take over the work. Your subconscious works day and night. It continues to seek a solution whether you are consciously thinking about it or not. In fact, practice suggests that the subconscious works better when left alone. We are more open to insights from the subconscious in moments when we are not thinking of anything in particular.

Any time you can spend just daydreaming and relaxing is useful in the creative process—a shower, long drives, a quiet walk, a hike in the forest. For example, Nolan Bushnell, founder of the Atari company, first conceived of what became his biggest-selling video game while walking alone on the beach one quiet morning. Steven Spielberg, on the other hand, reports that most of his best ideas come while he's driving the freeway. And Albert Einstein once remarked to a colleague, "Why do I always get my best ideas in the shower?"

Being overly concerned about getting the right answer can in fact hinder the process. It's like a professional athlete being too anxious about winning a championship game. Athletes know that to perform at their best they have to be focused but relaxed. As soon as they put too much pressure on themselves they make mistakes. For your intuition to work you have to relax and let it work.

AWAKENING THE INTUITION

Here are three steps that will naturally and effortlessly awaken your intuition and bring the answers you require:

Step 1

Spend several minutes thinking about the fact that you do indeed possess a powerful subconscious mind, that the perfect answers and solutions exist, and that your subconscious can and will access this information for you. Try to get beyond an intellectual understanding of this to where it becomes an emotional conviction. When this happens you will feel charged and excited. The conscious mind must be reminded again and again of the existence and potential of this hidden partner. You want to sense and feel this with assurance. Let your mind contemplate this great power you possess within.

Step 2

Clearly state what it is you wish your subconscious to bring to you—what answers, solutions, insights. Repeat to yourself a number of times that your subconscious mind is at this very moment working for you. Don't feel pressured or confused or try to figure out the answers. Speak to your subconscious with confidence, repeating over and over what you want it to do, but word it in such a way that it is already doing so. "My subconscious is now bringing me. . . ." Repeat this to yourself at least ten times, feeling that the process is already in motion.

Step 3

Relax and fill your mind with faith and expectancy that the correct answer will come to you. Remember, faith and confidence are not only attitudes, but vibrations of energy. These vibrations will attract the appropriate solutions and answers just as a magnet attracts metal filings. A mind vibrating with the belief that answers are coming to it naturally draws those answers. If you had the correct and perfect solution, imagine how you would feel: excited, overjoyed, relieved. Feel those sensations now. Let your mind play with this mood in a re-laxed way. Drop off to sleep with the assurance that the an-swers are soon to be yours.

This entire three-step process takes five or ten minutes and is best done each evening before you go to sleep. The twi-light period between conscious and unconscious levels is a most opportune time to reach the subconscious.

RECEIVING THE INFORMATION

Sometimes the answer will come as a hunch or insight that pops into your mind when you least expect it; perhaps, like Steven Spielberg, when you are driving your car, or maybe when you're eating your breakfast. At other times, the an-swer will come as the "still small voice within," the little voice or feeling that says, "Go here, try this, phone so and so."

Learning to pay attention to these feelings and hunches, and recognizing the voice within takes practice, but with time you will develop this ability. Don't be discouraged if you can't distinguish your intuition at first. Since most of us have not been taught how to recognize and use our intuition, it's only natural that we'll be a bit rusty at first. This ability is like a muscle and will get stronger and clearer with use. You strengthen your intuition by paying attention to it, looking for it, trusting and acting on it when you feel you hear it. First and foremost become aware of its existence, and begin to lis-ten within.

Have you ever taken a walk in the forest with an avid and

experienced birdwatcher? He or she will see ten birds to every one you notice. Their eyes are attuned. They know what to look for. Their senses are sharpened with practice. Exactly the same will occur with developing your intuition. Keep vigilant watch over and be sensitive to what's happening within you. You may miss it most of the time in the early stages, but soon you will hear and feel your intuition. It's closer to you than you can imagine. All it takes is a little trust and practice.

Frequently, intuitive ideas come to us in dreams. Dr. Frederick Banting, the brilliant Canadian physician, discovered the basics of insulin in a dream which instructed him in exactly what steps to take to find the elusive formula. Elias Howe, the inventor of the sewing machine, labored for years over its design, yet always remained one small detail from his goal. One night he dreamt he had been captured by savages who were pointing strange spears at him, and he noticed that at the tip of each spear was a hole. Howe awoke from his dream with the solution: put the hole at the tip of the needle! That simple change was the key that unlocked the invention of the sewing machine.

The methods the subconscious uses to bring you information will vary from one time to the next, but you will always know you are receiving intuitive information by the quality of the ideas, and by the feelings they produce within you. The exhilaration, the certainty, and the overpowering sense that "this is it!" are what distinguish intuitive ideas from all the other thoughts occurring in your mind.

STAYING OPEN TO INTUITION

Certain attitudes and behavior will encourage intuition, and these are worth cultivating. In many ways, we tell the subconscious mind what we expect from it, and we get what we expect. Acceptance and confidence create receptivity. If you can learn to think of your intuition as a normal and valuable part of daily living, and issue an open invitation to come at any time, it will show up bearing gifts. But thoughts such as, "I can't solve that problem," or "I'll never find the answer," signal the intuition not to bother. Confident thoughts, and the conviction that you deserve and expect not only an answer, but the best answer, stir intuition to positive action.

Don't be timid. Boldly tell your subconscious mind that its wisdom, knowledge and power are guiding and instructing you. At night I talk to my subconscious in the same manner that I would talk to a friend. I tell it (while simultaneously reminding myself) that it is all-powerful, that it has access to "Infinite Intelligence." I confidently instruct it in what I want it to accomplish for me. Then I rest in peace with full assurance that it will. It always does.

Here is an affirmation you may want to try:

"My subconscious mind is my partner in success."

If you break this affirmation down, you will see that it contains three powerful elements:

1. "My subconscious mind . . . " By affirming this you acknowledge to yourself that you do indeed have a subconscious mind. You are recognizing and accepting your "unseen partner" as real. You are reminding yourself again of its existence, and it is impossible to remind yourself too many times. You want to permanently imprint this truth within you.
2. ". . . is my partner. . . ." A partner is someone who works side by side with you to achieve a common

goal, someone with whom you split the workload, each of you tackling different problems. Why not let your subconscious partner specialize in the task to which it is best suited—namely supplying you with accurate information, ideas and answers? You are never alone, never without guidance, because you can always count on your subconscious mind. It supplies the ideas; you supply the action.

3. "...in success." The word "success" is a powerful affirmation representing everything you want to see happen to you in business, in relationships, and in life. Just the act of repeating the affirmation sets vibrations of energy in motion that will greatly assist you in achieving your goal.

WHAT TO DO WHEN YOU NEED TO MAKE A DECISION IN A HURRY

Sometimes we need to make a quick decision. We can't wait weeks; we need the answer this afternoon. When you need to make a decision in a hurry, try this technique:

Relax your body with some deep breathing or just shrugging and relaxing your shoulders. Feel calm and relaxed. Quiet your mind and then confidently affirm to yourself ten or twenty times, "I always make the right decision." Feel the power of the words. Say them with assurance, and as you finish your last affirmation immediately make the decision. In this way you bypass the logical mind and let your intuition supply the answer. The first thing that comes to you will be your answer.

It is sometimes valuable to know how to bypass the logical mind. When we live too logically, we are out of sync with life. Life is not always logical. It is filled with paradoxes and mystery. That is why it's important to trust our intuition, feelings and hunches. When we do this we are closer to the truth than when we dogmatically remain within the narrow confines of our rational mind.

Unfortunately, schools don't teach us to trust our intuition. Instead they teach us to sort and decipher hard knowledge. But in real life, you find that even after you gather all the relevant information, there is still a gap, a part that you cannot neatly calculate. That's where you can add your intuition to make your final decision, and then act.

The quality of your life depends upon the quality of your thoughts and ideas. How many times in the past have you fruitlessly searched your mind for solutions, going over the same information time and time again in the hope that you've missed something? The answers weren't there because by searching only your conscious mind you greatly limited your possible solutions. By using the same tired, worn-out ideas you've been hashing and rehashing for years, you have put a blindfold on yourself and tied one hand behind your back. No wonder you were not succeeding to the degree you desired. The subconscious mind contains new ideas, answers and solutions in abundance. Don't limit yourself. Go to the treasure house within and bring back something new and dynamic that is full of life and spirit and originality. These ideas and solutions exist right now within you.

Once you recognize the omnipotent power that exists in the subconscious mind, you will never want for answers. You will merely adjust your consciousness and direct your intuition to bring you the required information. As the Upanishads say, "All exists within."

N I N E
Dreams

Dreams will show you where you are and where you are going. They reveal your destiny.

—Carl Jung

Dreams have fascinated and intrigued mankind since the beginning of time. The oldest written record of dream interpretation is to be found in the Babylonian *Epic of Gilgamesh* recorded on clay tablets in 3000 B.C. We know that the ancient Greeks and Egyptians practiced "dream incubation," where dreams were artificially stimulated by suggestion in temples or sanctuaries devoted to healing. The Bible contains numerous references to individuals being guided by dreams. Joseph predicted for the Pharaoh seven years of feast followed by seven years of famine by correctly interpreting a dream. In the Aztec hierarchy of gods the highest and most respected god was the bringer of dreams. The North American Indians had dream lodges where the elders of the tribe would interpret dreams received during visions and ceremonies, and make decisions based upon their interpretations.

Until recently most people in modern society dismissed this aspect of our psyche as unimportant, and as a result lost a vital source of guidance and connection to the inner self. Fortunately, this is now changing as individuals in growing numbers pursue this rich source of meaning and understanding in their lives. What makes dreams so interesting is that dreams are where the conscious and subconscious meet, where the images of day-to-day living encounter the hidden wisdom of the subconscious.

Many scientists first dreamt of solutions to problems they were struggling with, only later working them out consciously. Einstein dreamt he was riding on a beam of light long before he developed the theory of relativity. Numerous artists, businessmen, researchers and men and women of all walks of life are guided to creative solutions in their dreams. Certainly there is now enough evidence to suggest to even the most skeptical that there is more to dreams than just meaningless random images.

I wrote in the previous chapter of Dr. Banting and Elias Howe who made their breakthrough discoveries through the aid of their dreams. Let me add another example to this growing list.

Nobel Prize–winner Dr. James Watson was led to discover the enigmatic properties of the DNA molecule through a dream he had one night. He had been working on trying to understand the molecular construction of DNA for years, to no avail. One night he had a dream in which he saw two snakes coiling around one another. He woke up instantly and exclaimed, "I wonder if that's it? I wonder if DNA is a double helix twining around itself?" This form did not exist anywhere else in nature. He followed this trail and it indeed led him to decipher the enigmatic genetic coding for which he was awarded a Nobel Prize.

Dreams are the forgotten language of our race, and within their strange symbols and allegories are hidden meanings and messages that can guide and instruct us if we can learn to decipher them. I have studied and analyzed my dreams for a number of years now, and by observing my dreams over this extended period of time and attempting to interpret them, I can say with certainty that they reflect a superior intelligence, a wisdom which speaks to us. Our dreams show us where we are wrong and where we are unadapted, bringing to our attention the root cause of inner disharmony or emotional distress. They reveal a deeper meaning in our lives and consistently and regularly convey illuminating insights. Dreams show us how to fulfill our destiny, how to realize the greater potential of life within us.

We dream an average of five to seven times a night. This might surprise you, as perhaps you feel that you seldom dream, but in fact everyone dreams every night, whether we remember those dreams or not. We know this because when we dream we exhibit "rapid eye movement," a phenomenon which psychologists and scientists can measure, thereby determining how often we dream.

Babies are dreaming about 50 percent of the time they are asleep; premature babies 70 percent. We dream more frequently after days full of worry and stress, after intense learning experiences, after traumatic events or new and stimulating experiences, suggesting perhaps that dreams are important in helping us cope with changes in our lives.

PROGRAMMING YOUR MIND TO DREAM

1. Inform your mind just before you go to sleep that "tonight I will dream and I will remember my dream." Repeat this to yourself about twenty times.

You can even suggest what it is you wish to dream about, what area you wish to explore, but remember that dreams often have their own agenda. They know better than we what we need to understand.

2. Place a pad of paper and pen by your night table. This is symbolic as well as functional. You are demonstrating your willingness to explore your dreams. Your attitude towards dreams determines their attitude towards you. As you prepare for dreams, respect and acknowledge them. Doing so will cause them to more readily come to you.

3. Upon awakening don't leap out of bed, but remain still as your consciousness returns. This in between time is very valuable. It is the crack between the two worlds. Is there a shred of a dream vaguely fluttering around in there somewhere? If so, observe it like a hunting dog silently watching its prey. Try to bring as much of it back as possible, piece by piece. Rerun the dream in your mind several times, adding detail each time. Keep doing this till you have reconstructed as much detail and story as you can. Now rise and write down your dream, adding more detail as it comes to you. Once the dream has been recorded, you can begin to interpret it or leave it and return to it later.

DREAM INTERPRETATION

When interpreting your dreams an attitude of intense interest, rather than one of frivolous curiosity, will assist you. Think of yourself as an explorer in a new land, or an archeologist digging up clues at an ancient site. In many ways dream interpretation is like the work of an archeologist; not only do you have to find the relics but you must interpret what they are and what they mean.

The dream mentioned previously in this chapter, and the dreams in the chapter on the subconscious, are all fairly easy to understand and I used them because they clearly illustrate how dreams can guide us. However, because they are so easily decipherable, they are the exceptions. Ninety percent of your dreams will make little or no sense whatsoever. They will seem like nonsense, like a foreign language that you don't understand. However, if you're willing to work with your dreams, and you understand some of the keys to deciphering them, they will open up an exciting new world for you.

Dreams use the vocabulary of symbols and allegory to convey their message. Symbols are to intuition what words are to thought. The language of dreams is more like art and poetry than linguistics. Interestingly, one of the suggestions as to why our subconscious uses symbols rather than language is that this part of our consciousness predates language.

Your dreams are messages sent from your subconscious to you, and as such they are showing you something about yourself. Dreams are always about you and your circumstances—where you are stuck, what you're avoiding, what you're missing, what you're ignoring, where you need to go. Ninety-five percent of the time all the characters, creatures, monsters and strangers in your dreams represent aspects of yourself. When you go about interpreting a dream assume that all the people in the dream are you (except when you recognize the characters—children, spouse, parents, co-workers, and so forth—and even then they are sometimes you).

As an example, let's say you have a dream where a burglar breaks into your home and is trying to steal and harm your children. You confront the burglar and a life-and-death struggle ensues. You wake up.

Interpreting the dream subjectively, you would first of all assume that you are both the burglar and yourself in the dream. You begin asking yourself questions. What part of me is harming the children? Maybe you feel you're working too hard and not spending enough time with them. Is your dedication to working long hours perhaps stealing your children from you?

Another interpretation might be that your children are the carefree and innocent part of you, and the burglar is your serious and logical side. Is the "adult" part of you suppressing your natural, easy-going, more spontaneous nature? Perhaps your dream is telling you something is being taken from you by living too much this way. Get the idea?

Remember to avoid translating your dreams too literally. Say you dream you are driving a fast sports car at ninety miles per hour around dangerous curves. You lose control, crash and die. Does this mean you're going to have a car crash and die? Highly unlikely. It is far more probable that the dream is telling you something much less literal about yourself. Are you losing control of some part of your life? Where do you need to slow down? Perhaps the dream is suggesting that if you don't slow down you'll "crash," i.e. you'll get sick, lose something valuable, or alienate someone important to you. Death in a dream usually means change, transition, the end of one part of your life and the beginning of another. Are you heading for a change? Maybe a change is coming very quickly. Does any of this fit?

A nightmare is your subconscious trying to shock you into looking at some aspect of your life. It is as if the subconscious is saying, "Look here, this is urgent." Likewise, dreams that repeat themselves are messages trying to break through. When you correctly interpret them, they will cease. They are only continuing because you're failing to hear their message.

Here are a few techniques to apply when interpreting your own dreams:

- Name the dream. Give it a title. It doesn't matter whether the title makes sense or not, let your intuition come up with something. The title may give you some clues.

To illustrate how this might work, many years ago I was about to invest some money in a venture that looked like a unique opportunity. Shortly before we were to consummate the deal, I had a dream in which one of the partners was walking a skunk on a leash. I remarked, "What are you doing walking a skunk?" He shrugged it off as normal. I woke from the dream and tried to make sense of it. I gave the dream the title, "Something Stinks," and as a result, I decided not to invest. It looked like I was throwing away a golden opportunity, yet two years later all the parties involved were bankrupt. Listening to my dream saved me from losing my money.

- Go back into the dream during waking hours and speak to the dream characters. Find a quiet spot where you will not be disturbed for five or ten minutes. Closing your eyes, recreate the dream in your mind. See it happening exactly as it did the night before—the same scene and people. Project yourself back into the dream and let the drama unfold, only this time you can react in any way you choose. For example, in the dream where the burglar breaks into your house and tries to harm your children, recreate the dream exactly as it happened, except that when it comes time to fight the burglar, instead of fighting, enter into a dialogue. Question the burglar: Who is he? What does he want? Why is he doing this? What are you trying to tell me? Since you now control the dream, you can do this. Perhaps talk to your dream-children and ask them questions as well. You may be quite surprised at what they say. This technique can be invaluable in helping to make sense of it all. And yes, they will speak to you.

- Compare the dream to a drama and examine it under these structural headings:
  1. *Introduction.* The setting of the dream and the meaning of the problem presented.
  2. *The plot.* The action, the ups and downs of the story as it unfolds.
  3. *The ending.* How does it end? Was the problem resolved or unresolved? What message or theme is implied by the way the story ended?

In examining the dream in this way you should ask what the main symbols are. What might these symbols represent? What are my past associations with these symbols? How are they speaking to me now?

Examine, too, how do you feel in each part of the dream? This is a clue to its meaning. Do you feel relieved, terrified, confident, empowered? Perhaps you dreamt you witnessed a murder, but instead of being terrified and upset you were happy and excited. You woke up confused by this. The fact that you were happy and excited is the clue. What part of you or your life needs to change (be murdered)? Would you feel excited or relieved if there were changes in this part of your life? What changes may it be suggesting? Examine all the clues.

Sometimes dreams reveal themselves right away. Mostly they need germination time, a few days or weeks before they begin to make sense, and sometimes not even then. But even if you don't decipher every dream, (you'll be lucky in the beginning to decipher one out of four) the very act of working on your dreams allows for valuable growth and change within the subconscious. No work is without compensation on one level or another. Nor is dream interpretation something you can do with rational effort alone. One depends as much on intuition as on logic.

Every dream remembered and correctly interpreted makes a lasting connection. One is forever linked with it, and through that dream one is linked with one's inner center. When our interpretation hits the mark, something inside us clicks. We say, "Yes, that's it." We feel empowered. Whenever we understand a dream properly, it is nourishing, something becomes peaceful and satisfied within us. We have gained direction and insight from within. Dream interpretation is always a living dialogue with our own subconscious. With practice we come to know that we are connected to something powerful and infinite within us.

Reality

*Man has his future within him,
dynamically alive at this present
moment.*

—Abraham Maslow

What is happening right now in your life is not happening to you as a result of chance. Your past consciousness has helped to create it. Your "now" has its causes and roots in the past.

Consider the following analogy: When you look up into the sky and see the stars, what you are actually seeing is the past because some of those stars may no longer exist. This is possible because stars are hundreds and thousands of light years away, meaning that it takes their light, traveling at 186,000 miles per second, hundreds or thousands of years to reach the earth. Thus, the light we see from a star a hundred light years away is actually light it emitted a hundred years ago. That particular star could have exploded and disintegrated twenty-five years ago, but we still see its light, and will continue to see its light for another seventy-five years, even though the star itself has long ceased to exist.

Keep this analogy in mind when using mind power techniques to change your reality, for when you begin to change your thoughts, your new reality will not immediately follow. There will always be a certain time lag during which you will be in a position of developing a new consciousness, but still stuck with your old reality.

This "waiting for it to happen" period is critical, because how you react during this waiting period will either quicken or hinder the new reality you are attempting to create. You may doubt things are changing. You may feel discouraged and wonder if you are wasting your time. Your mind will try to fool you by telling you that nothing will happen, that this won't work. These thoughts are natural; they happen to us all. Do not pay them any heed; just continue with your exercises, being patient and diligent in your efforts. It helps to remember that reality is a process, a continuous happening, and not something fixed and rigid.

Everything in existence is continually in the process of becoming something else. Your circumstances, too, are forever changing and becoming something else, so how could your new thoughts, if persisted in, do anything but bring you a new reality? Think about it.

Relax and enjoy your exercises, ignoring any negative thoughts. In time your life will change naturally and effortlessly. You don't have to force it.

KEEP THESE POINTS IN MIND

1. Be conscious of what you are thinking. You are creating your future experiences with your "now" thoughts.
2. Change your reaction to any undesirable conditions in your life. If you are struggling in your career,

without a relationship, sick, unemployed, or nothing seems to be working for you, the first thing you must do is accept the situation. Don't try to pretend it isn't happening. It is. Don't waste time feeling sorry for yourself or fighting it; work through it with mind power.

3. Establish a daily inner "creating" period for yourself free from everyday demands and distractions. It is this inner creating period that will give you power.

I once called a company to get some important information which I needed for my business. The woman I spoke to asked me to call back in half an hour, explaining, "I'm sorry. We can't get into our computer right now; it's running a program." I put down the receiver and thought to myself, "That's exactly how we practice mind power. When we run a mental program we close off our mind to all outer distractions and run our program over and over again in our mind."

CHANGE IS A CUMULATIVE PROCESS

Imagine you have an eyedropper full of red dye and every day you squeezed one drop of dye into a large bowl of water. At first you would see no effect, because the dye would quickly dissipate and be absorbed. If, however, you continued to add a drop every day, the water would gradually turn from clear to pale pink, to deep rose, and finally to brilliant red.

In creating a new reality for yourself your "eyedropper" is that daily creating period during which you detach yourself from your worries, your difficulties and your "now" reality. This period can be anything from five minutes to thirty minutes, so long as you observe it every day. By regularly and diligently applying the techniques you have learned, an ever-increasing effect is seen. Those who practice half-heartedly soon fall by the wayside, but nothing is beyond the reach of those who have vision, understanding and commitment.

Will you dare to believe in your vision as being stronger and more potent than your present circumstances?

Are you willing to infuse yourself daily, without fail, with thoughts of your desired reality?

Will you persevere, trusting in your daily practice and refusing to believe otherwise, even in the face of seemingly unchanged or contradictory conditions?

If you can, then you shall have whatever you desire. You will step forward boldly into the world, and the world will give you whatever you ask of it.

Concentration and Contemplation

To fully understand a grand and beautiful thought requires, perhaps, as much time as to conceive it.

—Jean Joubert

Most people have an erroneous idea of what concentration is. They associate it with hard work and sometimes painful school memories, convincing themselves in the process that concentrating is difficult. If, however, you've ever lost yourself in the enjoyment of a movie or concert, you've found that concentrating actually comes quite naturally when you are absorbed in something that you enjoy.

Concentration requires no superhuman effort. But it does require practice. It is a skill that is learned and developed and like most skills the more you use it, the easier it becomes. In fact, as you develop your powers of concentration, not only will you find it progressively easier to direct your thoughts towards whatever purpose you have chosen, you will also find your own mental clarity and powers of insight greatly enhanced.

The ability to concentrate and focus your mind on one idea, thought or image is a prerequisite for using mind power. Unfortunately, if we have never trained our mind, we will probably find that it is very unruly and active, moving from thought to thought with very little attentiveness. This is one of the first things we notice as we begin to train our mind. Our mind is more restless than we realized; there is effort and willpower needed to direct it. And direct it is exactly what we must learn to do—direct it to think the thoughts we choose, and reject the thoughts we wish dismissed. For so long as we yield to every single thought within our mind, letting each one take us along for a ride in whatever direction it goes, we remain caught within our fantasies, our worries, our tendencies toward avoidance. Each and every thought holds us in its powers. Learning to concentrate is regaining control. Steadying the mind through various concentration techniques disciplines and strengthens the mind. And this in turn allows us to exercise discretion with regards to the thoughts we are thinking.

Developing your concentration is like developing and strengthening a muscle. If, for example, you haven't been to the gym for a while you'll find your first workout torturous, difficult, unpleasant. But if you continue working out every day or every second day, following a regular routine, you will soon find it enjoyable and pleasant. Not only that but you will feel good and see a noticeable change in your stamina and physical appearance. It's the same with working out in the mental gym of your mind. Your mind is not used to disciplined thinking, so your first few attempts at trying to concentrate will be met with resistance, and obviously will not be nearly as productive as after you have been mentally working out for a while. This is important to remember; don't be discouraged by what happens your first few times. Be patient with yourself and give yourself time to develop these new skills. It's steady and regular practice that ensures the best results. And the results will come, I assure you.

CONTEMPLATION

The technique of contemplation is the single best way I know of for developing your powers of concentration. And not only will it sharpen and strengthen your mind, but it will also give you greater insight into whatever it is you are exploring. The practice of contemplation forms an integral part of our training.

With contemplation we break through the surface ideas, truths, laws, whatever it is we are contemplating, to explore their deeper meaning and implications. This is how all great artists, inventors, mystics and visionaries throughout the ages have received their insights. Without deep contemplation it is almost impossible to pierce below the mystery of things, and that is why most people have only a surface understanding of their reality. How often do we fool ourselves into believing that because we can quote facts or make intelligent arguments about a subject we know everything there is to know about it? We may know something about it, but that something may be a very little piece of the whole picture, and it certainly doesn't mean we "know" it at all.

Let me give you an example. Consider the difference between a tomato picked while still small, hard and green, and one allowed to sun-ripen to its sweet, juicy fullness. You could say you know what a tomato tastes like after having eaten the green one and technically you would be right. You could argue that tomatoes are bitter and hard, as that is your experience with tomatoes. But now you sample the luscious vine-ripened one, and you immediately see how much you missed. Your awareness of the possibilities of "tomato" has just broadened immensely. You have now tasted both stages and now you know the difference. The true potential of a green tomato has been revealed to you. Likewise, you could say, after reading this book once, that you now understand how mind power works, and it is true you have received the basic information. But how different it is for an individual to not only read the book but to practice regularly the techniques suggested. This person will have a far greater capacity to know and understand the powers of the mind than someone with mere intellectual or factual knowledge. Likewise, a person who contemplates any subject for a period of time will have a far deeper understanding than one who does not.

HOW TO PRACTICE CONTEMPLATION

Contemplation is using your mind like a searchlight to seek out new information. It is to take up one idea, thought, law or truth and probe it deeply. It is disciplining your mind to remain focused on whatever it is you're contemplating as you rearrange its contents, thinking them over, establishing new relations, discovering hidden likenesses and previously unthought of connections.

You may contemplate anything that inspires you, or something that you wish to understand more clearly. For example, let's say you wish to contemplate the idea that thoughts are real forces. Using a watch or clock to time yourself (I suggest five minutes minimum and ten minutes maximum per contemplation exercise), begin to focus on "thoughts are real forces." Lose yourself in the idea, thinking deeply about it. Ask yourself questions such as, "What does this mean? What are its implications? How does this affect me? Can I make this work for me?" Maintain your contemplation for the allotted time; don't allow your mind to wriggle out of the experience.

During your contemplation, if your mind wanders (and it will wander), gently but firmly bring it back to the subject of your reflections. In the beginning stages of practicing contemplation your mind will probably drift off ten or twenty times in a five-minute period. Totally irrelevant thoughts will come to your mind in the middle of your practice. Memories of recent events, thoughts of tasks waiting to be done, desires, worries and fantasies will enter uninvited and try to hold the field of your attention. Do not let this distract you from your exercise. As soon as you become aware of the intrusion, dismiss it and begin again at the point where you left off. Your mind is not accustomed to being disciplined and directed in this way. It would rather meander freely and focus on whatever it chooses. Your mind will become bored and feel there is nothing more to think about. It will become restless. Ignore all these feelings and simply bring your mind back again and again to your central theme, pressing on with this inner inquiry for the prescribed time. This is true mental gymnastics and excellent training. You are now directing and controlling your mind, rather than the other way around.

As you continue to do this exercise over a number of days and weeks, two things will happen. First of all, by disciplining and exercising your mind in this way you are developing your powers of concentration. This will make you more alert and creative. And secondly, your limited intellectual understanding of what it is you're contemplating will deepen. You will find that during the exercise you will sometimes experience a sense of excitement and enlightenment as the truth comes alive within you. It is a good idea to keep pen and paper handy when contemplating, so you can write down any new insights as they come to you. You will find yourself experiencing an emotional level of acceptance of what you're contemplating, and this is far more gratifying and powerful than any simple intellectual understanding. You will penetrate deep into the heart of that subject.

The latent power of the mind is developed by exercise. The ability to think correctly and powerfully comes with practice. Begin today to strengthen your powers of concentration by practicing contemplation. You may choose to contemplate the notion that you possess a powerful subconscious mind, or that thoughts influence reality, or any other of the hundreds of life-changing principles contained in this book. But whatever you choose to contemplate, the rewards awaiting your efforts are myriad.

TWELVE
Beliefs and Imprinting

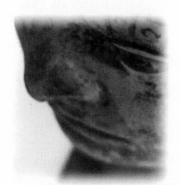

All truly wise thoughts have been thought already thousands of times; but to make them truly ours we must think them over again honestly, till they take root in our personal experience.

—Goethe

There is no area of our life about which we don't have a set of beliefs and assumptions, some of which we accepted way back in early childhood and have defended ever since. Once acquired, we rarely question these beliefs. We naturally assume they are all true; why else would we have them? If we think it's hard to make money, it's because it *is* hard to make money. If we feel we are worthless, it's because we *are* worthless. If we think there are no opportunities for us, it's because there *are* no opportunities. We will doubt and scrutinize almost all aspects of ourselves and our life, but our beliefs are always the last to be challenged.

WHAT YOU BELIEVE IS WHAT YOU GET

Most of us have unwittingly used our beliefs against ourselves many times. If you look at any of your problem areas you'll probably find they are rooted in faulty and limited beliefs. So if you are having problems with your relationship, examine your beliefs about relationships. All your beliefs. Likewise, if you are having problems with health, look at your beliefs about health; if you are having financial problems, look closely at your beliefs about money.

After one of my lectures, a soft-spoken man in his mid-thirties confided to me that he had difficulties in making money. He always had just enough to support himself and his family, but never enough to save and get ahead. "I'll never have enough money," he shrugged, "It's impossible to get ahead."

These two negative beliefs, "I'll never have enough money" and "It's impossible to get ahead," lodged deep in his subconscious mind, were continuously at work coloring this man's reality. I suggested to him that these might not be the only limiting beliefs he held about money for, in my experience, most limiting beliefs drag a host of undesirable relatives along with them.

I asked him to write down all his beliefs about money and success. The resulting list was quite revealing. It included such commonly held beliefs as: "If I accept money from someone then they will go without," "There are no good opportunities left to make money," "Money is hard to make," "Successful people are selfish and I don't want to be selfish," and "I would have to give up too much to become success-ful." Quite a self-limiting and self-defeating list!

No wonder this man couldn't get ahead financially—he was at war with his own subconscious, battling a litany of beliefs which kept telling him he would have to become selfish, take from others, and give up too much in order to make more money.

At another of my lectures, a woman who had suffered constant poor health found, upon examining her beliefs, that she was telling herself: "Everyone gets sick," "There is so much disease around," "I catch everything," "My body is frag-ile," and "Disease is much more powerful than health." Luck-ily, she was able to eventually turn her health around, by adopting new life-strengthening beliefs.

The contents of your subconscious mind are of immense concern to you. If your subconscious mind has picked up worry, negativity, or limiting suggestions, it will accept them as true and will work with that belief day and night, ulti-mately bringing about the corresponding situations. If it be-lieves in poverty, failure and trouble, then your subconscious will endeavor in a thousand different ways to manifest those realities. What is contained in your subconscious mind, and the experiences you encounter in your life are directly con-nected to one another.

HAVE YOU SWALLOWED ANY SNAKES?

There's an old Zen parable about a foolish peasant who was sent to visit his master's house. The master brought him into the study and offered him some soup, but just as the peasant was about to drink it, he noticed a small snake in his bowl. Not wanting to offend his master he drank it anyway, and within a few days fell so ill that he was brought back to the house.

The master again took him into his study and prepared some medicine in a small bowl which he then gave to the peasant. Just as the peasant was about to drink the medicine, he noticed another snake in the bowl. This time he pointed it out and loudly complained that this was the reason he was sick in the first place. Roaring with laughter, the master pointed to the ceiling where a large bow was hanging. "It is the reflection of the bow you are seeing," he said. "There is no snake at all."

The peasant looked again and, sure enough, there was no snake in his bowl, only a reflection. He left the house without taking the medicine and regained his health within the day.

When we accept limitations about ourselves and our world we have swallowed imaginary mental snakes. And they are always real . . . until we find out otherwise.

Once your subconscious mind has accepted a belief or idea, whether true or not, it will continually feed you thoughts to support that belief. Let's say you unconsciously believe that it is hard to establish a loving relationship. This belief, repeated to yourself, soon becomes imprinted on the subconscious mind. Once imprinted, it will feed your mind with thoughts such as, "I'll never meet someone I like," "It's impossible to meet a good partner," "Relationships never work," and so on. When you meet someone special your thoughts become, "He's probably not that nice," "Why bother trying? It won't work," or "She'd never be interested in me." Furthermore, your mind, convinced that "it's hard to have a good relationship," will magnify any incidents that support this belief, and will ignore or dismiss incidents which indicate the opposite. Our mind will distort our perception of reality to make it conform to our beliefs.

Think you are worthless? Or that it's hard to make money? Believe you are susceptible to poor health? Your mind will find irrefutable evidence to support those beliefs and will work overtime to manifest those realities.

On the other hand, if you believe that you are a winner, or that there's money to be made everywhere—if you believe in your own vibrant health—you'll find yourself surrounded by equally strong evidence supporting *those* beliefs.

CHOOSE YOUR BELIEFS WISELY

In almost all problem areas of your life, *you* are the problem and *you* are the solution. It may not seem that way, but you are encountering your resistance not from outside sources, but from inside yourself—from your beliefs. When new beliefs are accepted by your subconscious mind whole new realities will open up.

For example, let's say you believe that "it's hard to make friends." Holding this belief now excuses you from making friends: it's not your fault—it's hard! It's only logical and understandable that you don't make friends. Your belief deludes you into believing that your lack of friends has nothing to do with *you*.

If you change your belief to "it's easy to make friends," your telephone may not suddenly start ringing off the hook with dinner invitations, in fact you may not make even a few friends, but you will have changed your focus. Suddenly the problem isn't out there: the problem is with you. Once you take responsibility for your reality, you can examine what you need to change in yourself, and sometimes just that change of attitude will open up numerous possibilities.

As you continue to believe that it's easy to make friends you will find plenty of evidence to support this belief, and you will make whatever changes are necessary to take advantage of this newly emerging reality.

CHALLENGE YOURSELF TO GREATNESS!

Challenge yourself to create new, more supportive beliefs even if on the surface you don't believe them. Remind yourself that you can voluntarily plant in your subconscious mind any thought, idea or belief you desire, and your mind will accept it provided it is introduced with feeling and reinforced through repetition.

The mind is a creature of habit. If you have allowed limiting concepts to root there, you can crowd them out by constructing new and more supportive beliefs, and by practicing them until the old ideas have been replaced by the new ones. So do a mental house-cleaning. Change the furniture and paint the walls. It's time to toss out all those old limiting, self-defeating beliefs, however cherished, and replace them.

Check the following list carefully to see if you are in the habit of using even one of these sayings:

> I can't do it.
> I'll never get ahead.
> There are no opportunities right now.
> I've tried hundreds of times.
> It doesn't matter what I do.
> It's hard to get ahead.
> Something always goes wrong.
> It won't last.
> Life is hard.
> You have to work hard for everything you achieve.
> Nothing comes easy.
> This is not the right time for me.
> I don't know what to do.

If any of these sound familiar, begin immediately to imprint new, more supportive beliefs. Allowing ourselves to succeed means being willing to give up the excuses, the security, and the other "benefits" we have derived from failure. Millions of people are content to stay as they are and will make no attempt to change. They believe life is hopeless and difficult and have resigned themselves to this fate; nothing will shake them from it. But what about you?

EXPLORE YOUR POSSIBILITIES

Step 1

Pick an area of your life in which you are having difficulty—finances, relationships, sex, health, business, whatever. Write down all your beliefs about the area. Take your time and be honest. Don't write what you think you should feel or what looks good, write what you really feel deep down. When you have finished, examine the list and search for limiting beliefs. We are not interested in whether these beliefs are true or not, only in whether or not they're limiting. This process, if done honestly, can be quite revealing in and of itself.

Step 2

Beside each limiting belief write a newer, more supportive belief. For example:

Limited Beliefs	New Beliefs
There are no ways for me to make money.	There are many undiscovered ways for me to make money.
It is hard to meet people.	It is easy to meet people.

It is hard to make friends.	It is easy to make friends.
I'll never get ahead.	I'm bound to succeed.
I have no time to work on this project.	There will be lots of time to work on this project.

Using the imprinting technique which follows, impress these new beliefs into your subconscious mind. Stick to one or two new beliefs a month; don't try to do too much at one time. As the months roll by you will find you have a number of powerful new beliefs working for you.

IMPRINTING

The imprinting technique is simple; you've been using it almost since birth. You've used it to learn first your language, and then facts like the multiplication tables. You immediately know the answer to 6 x 6 or 8 x 7 because the answers have been imprinted in your mind through numerous exercises and repetition. Remember how many times you wrote and memorized your multiplication tables? You probably don't remember learning to read either, but you did so by the same method—continually repeating words and phrases and correcting yourself, or being corrected, when you mispronounced or misused them. Now you can speak your own language effortlessly, because it has been imprinted into your mind.

Like any other new information, ideas and beliefs must be imprinted in your mind before you can use them successfully and automatically. The thrill of a new idea cannot be sustained for long because inspiration, however strong, soon fades and disappears. However excited a person may be with a new idea, if he or she is unable or unwilling to follow through on the initial enthusiasm, inevitably that person will lapse back into the original position, the old ways.

When imprinting, use a combination of affirmations and contemplations. While repeating the idea to yourself, think about it. Make it real to yourself and ignore contrary ideas. The new concept is still a tender shoot; nurture it through its first struggling stages. Be vigilant, for without care your unruly old ideas, like mental weeds, will take over and crowd it out.

There is a necessary germination period before any new idea or belief will take root and flourish in our consciousness. This takes time. It does not happen by whipping past a new belief once or twice, or even ten or twenty times. True imprinting requires one to three months before its effects are firmly fixed in the mind. That's thirty to ninety imprinting sessions of five to ten minutes each day. Can you see why people who try to adopt a new belief by reading it once or twice are doomed to fail? "I've tried to believe it but I just can't," they say hopelessly. Yet how hard did they try?

You are trying to create new beliefs in your subconscious mind, and very often these new beliefs contradict the existing beliefs you now hold. It's simply not possible for your mind to incorporate any new belief unless you intend to imprint it daily for a month or two. Why waste your time and disappoint yourself with half-hearted attempts? Every new belief needs time and attention to flourish; anything less will not succeed. Now repeat after me:

Every new belief needs time and attention to flourish.
Every new belief needs time and attention to flourish.
Every new belief needs time and attention to flourish.

Get the message?

THIRTEEN
Self-Image

*Something we were withholding
made us weak until we found
it was ourselves.*

—Robert Frost

While most everyone would agree on the importance of a good, healthy self-image, few of us understand how to acquire one or realize how the one we now possess was created in the first place.

Our self-image is exactly what it says: an image we have of ourselves made up of ideas that we have formed over the years. Once this image becomes imprinted on the subconscious mind, it takes on a life of its own and we forget that it is something we have created, something which can be changed and altered.

Let us look closer at how a self-image is formed. In childhood, when our "worth" was first established, we accepted all kinds of ideas about ourselves. If our parents were loving and supportive, we most likely feel relatively good about ourselves; if our parents abused, ridiculed or belittled us, we may have a less positive self-image. As we grew up and moved away from our parents and out into the world of our peers and other adults, countless other experiences impressed themselves upon us. Unfortunately, if we have made a habit of dwelling upon life's inevitable disappointments, we may have made disappointment the central part of our overall image.

BUILDING A STRONG SELF-IMAGE

A car that is not maintained properly will inevitably become a wreck. A house that is not kept up will become run-down and dilapidated. Your self-image, likewise, must be maintained if you want it to be strong and vibrant. It is through ignorance and neglect that a self-image deteriorates. Take responsibility. Take care of your self-image as you would take care of yourself.

Life is full of temporary disappointments, heartaches, failures and problems, and if we are not careful these can easily drag us down. We need to regularly reinforce our self-image in order to keep it healthy. We can do this by setting up a regular program to feed our mind with positive, uplifting, inspiring thoughts about ourselves. We can even cheat a little and include thoughts that aren't yet true. Remember, your subconscious mind will accept any thought about yourself that you regularly think, true or not, and that idea will eventually become part of your self-image.

Three useful concepts can be imprinted which will immediately strengthen your self-image:

1. *You are unique.* No one else has your thoughts, your ideas, or your ways of doing things. Most people

think they are ordinary but don't *YOU* make that mistake. Don't just recognize your uniqueness; proclaim it through your actions and in your daily thinking. Feel good about being alive and being you. Carry yourself with the dignity you deserve and you put yourself at a very great advantage.

2. *You can do anything.* We forget that life affords us countless possibilities and choices, and we too often become bogged down in our day-to-day routines, losing sight of what can be done if we but put our minds to it.

> You can travel to any country.
> You can learn any language.
> You can start any business.
> You can learn to play any musical instrument.
> You can join any group.
> You can learn any craft.
> You can develop any trade.
> You can change careers.
> You can begin any project.
> You can think any thoughts.

What *can't* you do if you put your mind to it? You have programs already written into your vast computer mind that cover every possibility. I call them our holographic possibilities. A tomato seed has only one possibility and that is to be a tomato. A rose cannot do anything but become a rose. Its fate is locked into that one reality, but you have infinite potential. The seed of whatever you choose to be is contained within you.

3. *You have unlimited power.* Every day of your life, you wake up with limitless power at your disposal.

The power I speak of is the ability to choose your thoughts. Nobody tells you what to think or how to think. You, and you alone, determine what you do with this power. You can create, build and strengthen any area of your life.

YOU WILL BECOME WHATEVER
YOU CONSISTENTLY THINK ABOUT YOURSELF

Timid thoughts create a timid person.
Confident thoughts create a confident person.
Weak thoughts create a weak person.
Strong thoughts create a strong person.
Thoughts with a purpose create a person with
  purpose.
Visionary thoughts create a visionary person.
Thoughts of helplessness create a helpless person.
Thoughts of self-pity create a person filled with
  self-pity.
Enthusiastic thoughts create an enthusiastic person.
Loving thoughts create a loving person.
Successful thoughts create a successful person.

YOU are responsible for your own self-image and *YOU* are responsible for creating and maintaining it. Acknowledge yourself regularly. Visualize, seed and affirm positive qualities for yourself.

LOVE YOURSELF

Self-love is very important—not an "I'm better than you are," but a nurturing feeling that "I'm OK as I am"—a realization that you don't have to be anything other than what you are.

It is ironic that the moment you can accept yourself as you are, you can easily change yourself and become something different. So long as you dislike yourself it is difficult to change, for it is self-acceptance at the deepest level which frees us to move on. Take the pressure off. You don't have to be anybody other than yourself. Once you accept yourself, you can explore some of the other "selves" you might want to become.

SELF-CONFIDENCE

Insist on self-confidence. Settle for nothing less than a firm belief and conviction that you can, and will, succeed. If you have had an unfortunate childhood, put it behind you; you are here now and your future awaits. If you have failed previously, so what? The only thing that counts is what you now think and what you do with those thoughts. As your self-image becomes stronger and more confident, life's situations will become easier, for as you change, so does everything around you. It is entirely in your hands.

FOURTEEN

Creativity

All the arts we practice are apprenticeship. The big art is our life.

—M. C. Richards

When we think of creativity we usually think of writers, painters, poets, musicians—individuals who are active in the arts, but creativity is by no means limited to these callings. Running a successful business, innovative parenting, a fun and interesting life, all require equal and sometimes greater amounts of creativity. Creative and inspired moments are vital to everything we do in life—relationships, family, business, work and our community. Successful people who live their lives with confidence count on their creativity to constantly come up with new ideas to propel them through day-to-day challenges.

Are you creative? How you answer this question will determine many aspects of your life. How you view yourself, whether you trust your instincts, how you problem-solve and

come up with ideas and solutions, all depend on what your answer is to this question. Let me explain. Several years ago I became aware of a study conducted by a major corporation
concerned about the lack of creativity among its engineers. To
deal with this problem, a team of psychologists was brought in
to find out what differentiated the creative people from those
who were not. Company executives hoped that through the
psychologists' findings, methods could be found to stimulate
the less creative group. The psychologists conducted all kinds
of tests to try to reveal what separated those who were creative from those who were not. Was there a magic ingredient,
and if so what was it? They asked hundreds of questions cov-
ering everything from educational background, upbringing
and hobbies to favorite food and colors, likes and dislikes.
They probed beliefs, thoughts and attitudes, looking for the
elusive key. After several months of study and several hundred
thousand dollars worth of fees, the psychologists found what
they were looking for. There was indeed a key factor that separated the two groups: *THE CREATIVE PEOPLE THOUGHT
THEY WERE CREATIVE AND THE LESS CREATIVE PEOPLE
THOUGHT THEY WERE NOT*. While this may in some ways
seem obvious, it is actually starkly revealing in understanding
who we are and how we live our lives.

What was happening with the engineers is that those who
believed they were not creative never allowed themselves to
explore new and different avenues. Why bother when you
have nothing to contribute? They simply felt they didn't
have the ideas and capabilities to be innovative. On the other
hand, those who thought they were creative acted accordingly. They regularly and consistently tried new approaches
and came up with new ideas and solutions, which in turn further supported their belief that they were indeed creative.

So you can see the importance of the question, "Are you

creative?"; whatever you answer will become a self-fulfilling prophecy. If you answered yes, congratulations. With the techniques presented in this chapter you will learn to become even more creative. If you answered no, don't despair. No matter what you presently think of yourself, you do have incredible creativity within you, all you have to do is awaken it. By practicing a few simple techniques you will discover your creativity, and it will assist you to succeed at your goals and dreams. Soon you will not only possess creativity, but you will come to value it as one of the most important tools of your life.

We all possess creativity. It's our nature to be creative. It is part of who we are. Unfortunately, many of us were told at some early age that we were not creative, and we believed it. As a result our creative instincts became repressed. Luckily they can be reawakened and harnessed again easily.

SIX CREATIVE TACTICS FOR A SUCCESSFUL LIFE

1. *Be an explorer.* It's one thing to be open to new ideas; it's quite another to actively seek them out. An explorer is forever trying novel and different ways of doing things. An explorer believes that there are new worlds, options, products, services, friends, methods and ideas waiting to be discovered. An explorer will venture off the beaten path. Most significant advances in art, business, education and science have come from someone exploring areas no one thought to investigate before. Explorers are not afraid of the unknown. They know that success and happiness come not from following others, but in finding your own unique way. So they forge ahead, always on the lookout.

2. *Ask questions*. Question everything. The word question is derived from the Latin word *quarerere* (to seek), which is the same root as the word for "quest." A creative life is a continued quest. Asking probing questions is indispensable to growth. Don't take anything for granted. "Be naïve, question everything," said prolific inventor Buckminster Fuller. There are no dumb questions. The only dumb question is the one you didn't ask. So question everything:

> Why am I living like this?
> Why am I doing this job?
> Where have I restricted myself?
> Where do I need changes?
> Why do I have toast and coffee for breakfast every day?
> Why am I not exercising?
> How can I spend more time with my family?
> Why do I always go to the same restaurant?
> What talents have I been neglecting?
> What habit, if adopted and practiced every day, would revolutionize my life?
> I wonder what would happen if I approached this person/client/company?
> I wonder what would happen if we halved/doubled our product line?
> I wonder what would happen if I stopped watching television?
> I wonder what would happen if we sold our house and moved to Mexico?

I have a friend who did just that. He asked himself that last question and liked the answer he received. He was married, with two young children and a promising career, but he and his wife sold everything and moved to Mexico. His parents and most of his friends thought he was crazy, irresponsible, especially with two young children, but this didn't stop him and his wife. They picked a quaint Mexican village known for its artistic community, and they moved there. He wrote his novel; his wife took up pottery, and the children adjusted to their new lifestyle. They spent almost four years in Mexico before eventually moving back again. While his novel never became a bestseller, he nonetheless followed his instincts and now works at a publishing house and is much happier than he was at his previous occupation. "It was the most daring and best move I ever made in my life," he says with a broad grin on his face.

It is essential not to censor yourself no matter how impractical or outrageous the question or answer sounds. This allows for fresh unanticipated insights to reveal themselves. If you're honest and open with yourself and diligently ask questions about every area of your life, you'll probably discover that some of these questions reveal blind spots and assumptions that deserve to be challenged. Others will open up needs and desires you've repressed. We are creatures of habit. We easily fall into routines that may have once served us well but now may be holding us back and keeping us in a rut.

Our future depends directly upon how well we question and examine our beliefs, actions, values, goals and ways of living. Asking the right questions is crucial for a creative life. If we want fresh perspectives and new insights, then asking penetrating questions of ourselves, and listening nonjudgmentally to the answers, will reveal untold creative opportunities for change.

3. *Get lots of ideas.* "The best way to get a good idea is to get lots of ideas", said Linus Pauling, Nobel Prize–winning chemist. If you have only one idea,

one solution to the problem you are facing, then
you have only one course of action. That's risky in
a world where flexibility is a requirement.

The one-answer, one-solution approach becomes deeply
ingrained in our thinking. Too often when we look for a solution or answer, we take the first one that comes to us.
Train your mind to look for many solutions. Allow your creativity and imagination to open up. "Yes, that works," you
say, "but maybe there is an even better answer." Looking for
the second, third and fourth solutions stimulates the creative imagination. Quite often, it's the second or third solution, the one that's a little unusual, that is exactly what suits
our purpose.

Guy Bouchard runs a successful advertising agency in
Montreal. He is paid to come up with innovative campaigns
for his clients. He has a rule which he says has served him
well in his career. "I force myself to always come up with at
least three different concepts for every campaign, and then I
pick the best. I'm often tempted to break the rule," he says.
"Sometimes I'll have what I think is a brilliant campaign on
my first idea. But I put on the thinking cap and come up with
two more, even if I'm positive that it's the first one I will use.
Sometimes it is the first idea I use, but more often than not
it's the second or third we end up running with."

Whenever you find yourself thinking that you've only one
option available to you, remind yourself that you are not being creative. Life is filled with numerous choices and options.
Open up your options by opening up your thinking. Train
yourself to find alternate solutions and options.

4. *Break rules—break habits.* Being creative often
    means breaking out of old patterns to create new

ones. There is no particular virtue in doing things the way they have always been done. Sometimes breaking rules, initiating a revolution in our life and overthrowing the tired habits and patterns that are keeping us stagnant is the most sensible way to go.

Scotty Bowman is well known in hockey circles as an innovative coach. He knows how to get the best out of his players. He won coach of the year in 1996 for leading his team, the Detroit Red Wings, to the most victories in a regular season, breaking the old National Hockey League record. He also has more wins than any other professional hockey coach and surpassed the astounding 1,000-win mark in February 1997. When his team is not playing well, Scotty will often shake things up by putting players together who are not used to playing with one another. This contradicts the conventional wisdom that says you keep the same players on the same line because they know each other and can anticipate each other's moves. Scotty is not afraid of trying different and unorthodox combinations to gain results.

I learned an interesting technique from a successful clothing manufacturer in New York. "When I feel bogged down," she said to me, "I change my sleeping patterns. Instead of getting up at seven and going to bed at eleven, I get up at four and go to bed at nine. Just changing this pattern seems to stimulate new ideas and productivity."

I later tried something similar with great results myself. For a three-month period I arranged my life so that I had two distinct sleeping periods in a twenty-four-hour cycle. I would get up at 4 A.M. and work till noon, go to bed at 2 P.M. and get up at 6 P.M., then work till midnight before retiring to bed again. This allowed me to be incredibly productive, plus I had the added advantage of having two "morning" periods where I seem to be at my best. I also had many more dreams, or at least remembered many more.

If you're not obtaining the results you want in life, maybe you need to break some rules. What habits or patterns can you break? How can you shake things up? Where in your life do you need a revolution? Now is the time to lead the charge. Don't be afraid to stir things up. When the dust settles you're often better for it.

5. *Use your imagination.* Our imagination is not bound by real-world constraints. Our imagination knows no limits. Whatever your mind can conceive of and believe, you can achieve. Our creative imagination helps us to explore different options and envision numerous scenarios and outcomes. By harnessing this faculty we can change and improve our life.

Here are two simple ways of using your imagination to come up with innovative ideas:

• *Imagine how others would do it.* What qualities do you admire in people? Whom do you respect for creative achievement, persistence or vision? Pick a role model, someone you would like to emulate. It can be someone living or dead, someone you know well or have never met. Now imagine this person is in your position. This person is faced with your particular problem or challenge. Imagine this person actually in your body (the imagination is not bound by real-world constraints) and taking over your situation. He or she is now able to live your life.

What would he or she do? How would this person, for example; John F. Kennedy, Nelson Mandela, John Lennon, Mother Theresa, go about it? What assumptions would they bring in? What constraints would they ignore? What special twists could they bring to the situation? What expertise would they add? What innovative or revolutionary changes would they make? This process can be extremely valuable in moving us out of our self-imposed restraints and showing us options we hadn't considered.

- *Imagine this person conversing with you and advising you*. This technique gained notoriety in the summer of 1996 when Bob Woodward reported that First Lady Hillary Clinton used it to have imaginary conversations with former First Lady Eleanor Roosevelt. It was taught to her by the brilliant author and scholar Jean Houston at a Camp David retreat. It is a simple technique which involves imagining yourself having a "real" conversation with a person you respect and listening to what that person advises you.

Jean Houston also guided TV host Larry King through an imaginary conversation with his mentor, the late TV legend Arthur Godfrey. This was done live on the Larry King show in front of millions of viewers to demonstrate both the effectiveness and simplicity of the technique. Corporate executives and professional athletes alike use this mentoring technique to gain insights and inspiration. Does it work? Let's listen to what Napoleon Hill has to say.

Hill is author of *Think and Grow Rich* and shares how he would convene imaginary meetings with his "invisible counselors." He chose nine men whose lives and life works had been most impressive to him, people like Abraham Lincoln, Andrew Carnegie and Henry Ford, and, just before going to sleep at night, he would close his eyes and see in his imagination this group of men seated with him around his council table. It is worth noting that, at these imaginary meetings, Hill was no passive observer. In his own words, "Here I had not only an opportunity to sit among those whom I considered to be great, but I actually dominated the group by serving as chairman."

Although Hill has stated most emphatically that it was all in his imagination and he didn't really believe he was conversing with the men, nonetheless, the ideas generated through this process were very real, and they led him "into glorious paths of adventure and wealth." Using this system he successfully solved all the difficult problems confronting him and his clients, and it helped him to become a very wealthy man.

6. *Fill the well.* Filling the well means nurturing ourselves. We must learn to be self-nourishing, to be alert enough to consciously replenish our resources. The new 21st century person will learn to balance work and leisure more effectively. As the Zen saying goes, "The bow kept forever taut will break." This is a fact that we ignore at our peril. When you value your creativity you learn to stimulate the "muse within." Fun and diversity are great stimulators.

Most major achievers in this world have reported that they often made their biggest breakthroughs after taking time out for contemplation and reassessment. This is not hard to understand, because when you are idle your subconscious mind (the creative mind) advances full steam ahead.

It's almost always during these quiet times that brilliant new ideas come forth.

Filling the well means thinking fun not duty. Do something different, unusual, stimulating. Surprise yourself by moving out of your normal routine. Take up a new hobby or activity, maybe skiing, painting, glass-blowing, hang-gliding, water polo, gardening; whatever fills the well and nourishes you. A stimulated and excited mind is a mind more receptive to new ideas than a mind bogged down with details and deadlines. And if you feel a little guilty having all this fun, simply remind yourself that you are filling the well.

IT'S TIME FOR A PERSONAL RENAISSANCE

The first half of the sixteenth century was a time of intellectual and artistic rebirth in Europe. A surge of creativity propelled European society out of the Dark Ages into what some called a golden age—the Renaissance. It was the time of Leonardo da Vinci, Michelangelo and Raphael. Christopher Columbus had just discovered America. Vasco da Gama sailed to India, Cortez to South America. People's concepts and minds were expanding. There was a scientific revival. Copernicus discovered that the earth revolved around the sun, rather than the opposite. The printing press was invented. It was a time of extraordinary intellectual achievement and artistic vigor, and the influx of new ideas and cultures opened up people's minds everywhere.

As we rapidly approach the twenty-first century we too have an opportunity to enter our own personal renaissance. Never before in the history of mankind has an individual been exposed to such a diversity of ideas, changes and options. Old ways are rapidly giving way to new as we literally redefine the way we live our lives. To many this is a daunting and overpowering prospect, but it need not be. Our subconscious mind is successfully assimilating this new reality and will advise us of the opportunities opening up to us.

Creativity is a necessary skill for successful living. Fortunately it is a skill that can be developed, as it is innate within us. The creative spirit when awakened is much more than an occasional insight. It is the ability to regularly and consistently solve day-to-day problems in innovative and unique ways. It means going beyond the routine and conventional. It means tapping into the inspiration that is forever within us and flowing with ideas.

A personal renaissance awaits you. Discover and use the creative spirit within and it will transform your life into an exhilarating adventure.

FIFTEEN

No Problems, Only Opportunities

Who can tell what is good or bad luck?

—Zen saying

Most of us dream of the day when we won't have any more problems, when everything will be resolved and our lives will be "complete." But problems are an important and valuable part of our lives, and instead of trying to eliminate them, we should strive to understand exactly what they are.

Nothing happens by chance. We are a part of a universe that is forever giving us definite messages and signals, often in the form of problems. It is not an accident or coincidence that a particular problem is happening to you at any given point in your life; our difficulties are signposts waiting to be read. Ask yourself: What is the problem I'm experiencing telling me about myself? What is it telling me about my thoughts? Beliefs? Actions? Choices? Lifestyle? *What is this problem trying to tell me?* Look closely and see if you can find the real cause. If you always feel sorry for yourself or helpless when a problem comes your way, you'll miss the important messages it brings you.

BECOME AN ALCHEMIST

The medieval alchemist spent his lifetime trying to learn the secrets of turning ordinary base metals into gold. Much time and great fortunes were spent in this pursuit, to no avail. Medieval alchemy failed because its practitioners were looking in the wrong direction. The real alchemist is one who learns the secret of turning everyday situations into gold, who learns how to make every situation serve him. Problems and difficulties can be used as a springboard to deeper insight, and the real alchemist understands that there are no such things as problems, only opportunities.

NO SUCH THINGS AS PROBLEMS, ONLY OPPORTUNITIES

Once a person takes on this belief and works at finding the opportunities that are contained within each situation, the experiences that follow this simple change of attitude are quite startling.

Margaret Kelly, a woman who had attended my "Thought Dynamics" seminars, found an opportunity to practice this principle one day at work. She was the director of a huge nursing home and, together with her two assistants, managed the day-to-day affairs of over a thousand patients. If even one of her assistants was off sick it created havoc, so you can imagine the "problem" she faced one day when both called in sick. She panicked, until she remembered that "there are no such things as problems, there are only opportunities." Where is the opportunity here? Margaret wondered.

Then Margaret realized that she was always working through just her two assistants, and that she didn't really know some of the staff they worked with. She told herself, "I'm going to use this as an opportunity to get to know these other people." She spent the day talking and working with employees with whom she normally had little contact. She listened to their concerns and to the difficulties they were having which, in turn, led to a whole new and more effective way of administering certain duties. As Margaret Kelly later told me, "The day turned out to be a wonderful opportunity, and I accomplished so much."

I doubt Margaret Kelly would have been able to turn such a tense situation to her advantage had she dwelt upon her so-called problem. It was changing her attitude from, "I've got a huge problem" to "There are no such things as problems, only opportunities," which had enabled her to try the new course of action, producing such rich results.

Nancy Spencer was facing the biggest problem of her life when I first met her. She had been deserted by her common-law husband and left with three small children. She had no money, no marketable skills, and no immediate prospects. It seemed like an insurmountable problem until Nancy began reminding herself that there are no such things as problems, there are only opportunities. But where? She searched for over a week before she finally found the opportunity she was looking for.

She realized, upon examining herself, that she had always been dependent upon someone—first her parents, and then her common-law husband. She had always allowed other people to tell her what to do because she had very low self-esteem. Now, in the depths of despair, in a seemingly hopeless situation, she made a promise to herself. Nancy resolved to rise up and become a confident and successful person, for herself and for her children. She would use this crisis as a springboard to become a strong and independent adult.

I was pleased I had the opportunity of teaching Nancy the concepts covered in this book, for she was an avid student and worked regularly and persistently on her self-image, her beliefs and her goals. I watched her change before my very eyes, and saw her progress from taking her first menial jobs to opening her own wholesale flower business. Today she is a happy, successful, self-confident woman married to a warm and sincere man. They share a wonderful life together—all because Nancy believed that there are no such things as problems, there are only opportunities.

Become an alchemist in life and make every situation serve you. Remember that many times we complain about events which, in retrospect, were necessary for our growth and development.

One of the great examples of turning happenstance to an advantage came about when researcher Don Stookey accidentally left some treated glass in the furnace so long it turned white. Undaunted, Stookey creatively turned that accident into a benefit by continuing to experiment with the new substance and, when he found it could withstand searing heat, further refined and marketed his mistake as Corning Ware, a product now found in almost every home in North America.

Learn to see your stresses and struggles as challenges and opportunities, not liabilities or handicaps. Consider the story of entrepreneur Kathy Kolbe who was born dyslexic, unable to tell left from right or read the time on a clock without great difficulty. "My disability is one of the greatest advantages I have," she says, "it helped me become a student of the thinking process."

One day Kolbe took the plunge. With $500 of her savings

she launched a firm called Resources for the Gifted. She compiled a catalogue of available resources for intellectually gifted children and sent it out to 3,500 teachers. At first, orders only trickled in, and even when they began to flow, the first years were hard. She bought a warehouse, and the building caught fire. An employee embezzled money. Kolbe divorced her husband. In spite of everything, she never lost sight of her belief that there are no such things as problems, there are only opportunities. Today she grosses $3.5 million a year and Resources for the Gifted continues to grow.

American President Franklin D. Roosevelt was a paraplegic who had to be helped in and out of his wheelchair, yet he brought America out of the Great Depression and went down in history as one of the world's most respected and revered leaders.

Bob Hawke rose from the depths of alcoholism to become an important labor leader and eventually Australia's Prime Minister for four successful terms.

Wilma Rudolph was born poor and black in Depression-stricken Tennessee. When she developed polio at the age of ten, life didn't seem very promising to Wilma, yet she surmounted all these problems and went on to win three gold medals in track and field at the 1960 Rome Olympics.

Thirty years later, another potential Olympian was facing the crisis of her life. Gail Devers was training to compete at the 1992 Barcelona Olympics when she suddenly broke out in sores all over her body. No one seemed to know what it was. Finally she was diagnosed with Graves Disease, a condition that had doctors threatening to amputate her feet. She was within two days of losing her feet when she finally began improving. Overcoming this adversity, she went on to win the 100-metre race in Barcelona, and then, with a home crowd of 85,000 cheering her on, she repeated this amazing feat in Atlanta in 1996. "I wouldn't change a thing," said Gail looking back on her ordeal. "It was a blessing. It made me the person I am today. It made me a stronger, better person."

The founding director of a highly successful investment firm shared with me his secret for hiring top performers. "We don't hire any senior people here unless they've had at least one major failure in their life. We find that people become more committed and determined as a result. It makes for a better person."

What opportunities are waiting for you right now in your life? You will never know until you look for them. Very seldom do opportunities stand up and wave a flag at you; they more likely come disguised as problems or failures. But opportunities do exist in abundance for all of us and, if you are willing to open up and explore your "problems" with this new attitude, some exciting surprises await you. Your struggles and stresses are challenges and opportunities. As Arnold Schwarzenegger says, "I believe very much in the struggle."

SIXTEEN

Healing Ourselves

The mind is a great healer.
—Hippocrates

C an the mind play a part in determining a person's sickness or health? "What goes on in a patient's mind is often the key to whether he will get well," says Dr. Carl Simonton. Dr. Simonton is medical director of the Simonton Cancer Center in Pacific Palisades, California, and an internationally acclaimed physician. He talks enthusiastically about the results he is obtaining by treating disease with visualization techniques.

"We think people are now beginning to realize how much the mind and the physical body are intertwined. Now we know it is possible for the cycle of disease to be reversed. We know that the same pathways that are used to transmit negative things, like cancer growth, can also be used to transmit positive things that can eventually restore a person to health. We are talking about some major changes in the way people view all illnesses and how they can cure themselves." Dr. Simonton and his colleagues are doing more than just talking, for his clinic achieves substantially greater than average cure rates for cancer, and he travels the country teaching other doctors how they can do the same.

In the last twenty years, I have taught my mind power training seminars to over 100,000 people and I have seen incredible results, from people becoming multimillionaires to people winning major sports championships. These are impressive achievements, but most fulfilling of all for me has been my experience in seeing hundreds of people cure themselves of illness using these techniques. Let me introduce you to Martin Brofman. He can tell you his own story:

"At the age of thirty-four, I found myself in a hospital being told by my doctors that I had a tumor that was imbedded within the spinal cord. The tumor was malignant and I was diagnosed as terminal. I was told I had two months to one year to live. After several weeks of total despair, I decided to try and help myself.

"For fifteen minutes twice a day I began meditating. On an imaginary screen in my mind, I pictured my body and the tumor. Each time I saw the tumor, I imagined it just a bit smaller than the last time I saw it. It was all in my mind, after all. I could imagine it any way I chose. I imagined that I could see the cancerous cells being dispersed by my body's natural immune system, and I told myself that they were being passed out of my body each time I went to the bathroom. Whenever I heard an inner voice suggesting that I was not getting better, I would quiet it, insisting that I was, in fact, in a state of improvement. I repeated to myself over and over while in this meditative state, 'Every day in every way, I am getting better and better,' until I believed it.

"In addition to the meditation sessions, I decided to reinforce my feelings of improvement in other ways.

Each time I felt a strange sensation or pain in my body, instead of telling myself that it was the tumor growing, bringing me closer to my death, I told myself that it was 'energy' working on the tumor, shrinking it, making it smaller and smaller, making me better and better. I looked forward to the sensations that I had formerly dreaded.

"All during the day, every day, I reminded myself of all the ways in which I was getting better. I imagined that the food I ate was 'energized,' making me healthier and healthier. I reminded myself continually of all the people who loved me, and I affirmed to myself that this love was energy I could put to use, to strengthen the healing process even more.

"I had no way of knowing whether all of these techniques were working or not, but I decided that if I felt better, they just might be. I had increasing mobility and energy every day, just as I was telling myself.

"Two months after I began reprogramming my mind, I was due for an examination by my doctor.

"The doctor was amazed. He found no evidence of a tumor at all. He could not believe it. This is exactly what I had visualized his reaction to be. I drove home, laughing all the way, to tell my wife the wonderful news."

This is far from an isolated case. There are countless examples of health being restored using similar techniques.

I remember a time when I was saying this to a group of students and a woman stood up and shared this story:

"Ever since I was a little girl, I have always said to myself, 'I'm the type of person who never gets colds.' I've always said that to myself and you know what? I never get colds."

The minute she finished a well-dressed man in his fifties popped up. "This is very interesting," he said, "because, you know, for as long as I can remember, I've always said to myself, 'Every year I'm good for one or two colds.' I've always said that to myself and you know what? Every year I get one or two colds." We all laughed, yet there is an important lesson to be learned here.

In 1981, U.S. President Ronald Reagan was shot in the lung by an attempted assassin. This was quite a serious injury, especially for a man in his seventies, but I knew he would be all right the minute I read a report from a journalist who had interviewed the president on his hospital bed. Reagan had said, "Don't worry about me. I'm the type of person who always heals quickly." What a healing belief. How powerful. Do you remember how quickly he was back at work? Within days!

Now let me ask you a question. What do you believe about yourself? Are you the type of person who says, "If there's a flu around, I'll catch it"? Do you expect to contract colds and flus and illnesses, or do you believe you are the type of person who never gets sick? What you believe is going to happen has a powerful effect on what *does* happen.

In a set of experiments described by Jerome Frank, an authority on the placebo effect, you can clearly see how what you believe affects what happens to you. In Frank's experiments, test patients were given one of three different substances: a very mild pain-killer, a harmless but ineffective placebo, and a heavy dose of morphine.

When patients were given useless placebos but were told they were getting morphine, two-thirds reported their pain disappeared.

When patients were given morphine but told they were getting a very mild pain-killer, over half said they still had pain.

And when patients were given a harmless placebo which they had been told caused headaches in previous experiments, three-quarters of them developed headaches!

Whatever the patients believed was happening seems to have been more important than what was actually happening. Medical authorities had already recognized the placebo effect, but this experiment went even further, with some very interesting results. Unknown to the doctors, they too, were being deceived, and the results were astounding. When the doctors administered a placebo under the impression that it was morphine, its effect on the patients increased. The experiment was then reversed, and when doctors thought the morphine they were administering was a placebo, its effect on the patients diminished. Obviously, what the doctors believed influenced the results as much as what the patients believed. But how could this be? How could what the doctor thinks possibly influence the patient? Isn't it what the patient thinks that counts? Or could it be that the doctor somehow subconsciously transfers to the patient his expectation of how the drug would affect him? If so, this is something to remember when a friend or someone close to us is ill. Our own attitude can be a valuable source of healing for both ourselves and others.

THE BODY IS A HEALING MECHANISM

Your body is a miraculous self-healing mechanism built to look after anything that happens to it. When you cut yourself, white corpuscles instantly rush to the spot to fight infection while the platelets congeal the blood and seal up the cut. It all happens automatically; you don't have to do a thing. Your body already knows exactly how to repair itself.

When you eat, your body extracts nutrients from the food and dispenses them as energy to various parts of the body, as required. It then discards the rest as waste and, again, it all happens automatically. You don't have to think about it or direct it. Break your arm, and you go to the doctor and the doctor heals your broken arm, right? Wrong. No doctor has ever healed a broken arm in his life. The doctor can align the bones to make sure they are straight, and he can put the arm in a cast to keep them that way, but only the body can heal the broken bones.

Remind yourself often that your body naturally heals and repairs itself. Insert thoughts of health and strength in your mind and you encourage it to happen. Affirm to yourself: "My body is a healing mechanism."

A TWO-MINUTE HEALTH TONIC

Every day spend several minutes bathing in thoughts of health and strength. Send these thoughts into your bloodstream, your tissues, your cells. Imagine energy flowing through you. Experience your body as a miraculous healing mechanism. This exercise is an invigorating health tonic, and all it takes is two minutes of your day.

YOUR ATTITUDE MAKES THE DIFFERENCE

When you first find out that you have a disease or illness the initial response is to panic. The mind becomes paralyzed with fear and the greater the illness the greater the fear. Part of the problem is that we see our disease as an alien entity or a "thing" rather than as a process. Wallace Ellerbroek, a former surgeon turned psychiatrist, says it eloquently: "We doctors seem to have a predilection for nouns in naming diseases (epilepsy, measles, cancer, tumors), and because we use nouns as names, then obviously they are things—to us. If you take one of these nouns—measles—and make it into a verb, then it becomes, 'Mrs. Jones, your little boy appears to be measling,' or 'Mrs. Baker, you seem to be tumoring,' which opens both your mind and hers to the concept of disease as a process which comes and then goes." Certainly Dr. Ellerbroek's approach is a more accurate way to look at illness.

Dr. Kenneth Pelletier of Stanford University School of Medicine points out that the body can't tell the difference between a "real" threat and a perceived one. Our worries and negative expectations translate into physical illness because the body feels as if we are endangered even if the threat is imaginary. In other words, people who fear diseases are more likely to get disease because the body feels the effect of the fear itself.

This phenomenon has long been observed in the area of conception. A Boston project, for example, found a 60 percent miscarriage rate in women who got pregnant soon after losing a baby to Sudden Infant Death Syndrome. The report urged that such bereaved women "should wait until the body is no longer feeling the effects of grief." And how many times have you heard of childless couples trying unsuccessfully for years to have a baby until, finally, they give up and adopt a child? Within months the woman is pregnant. It happened once the pressure to have a baby had been lifted.

FUN AND JOY CAN HEAL

It is no secret that depressed people become ill more readily than happy, easy-going types. Research has shown that stressful mental states like greed, anxiety, worry and fear can hinder the immune system's functioning. To combat this, several enlightened hospitals have set up "humor rooms" stocked with funny books, records, videos, cartoons and movies which patients can enjoy.

Recent medical research into humor and health has shown that laughter releases two important types of hormones from the brain, enkephalins and endorphins, which relieve pain, tension and depression. "There have been all kinds of reports in both folk and professional literature about people who have been cured or at least helped by the use of laughter and humor," says Shirley Routliffe, a Hamilton, Ontario therapist. Today, even traditional health professionals are making use of these findings.

EVERYONE IS DIFFERENT

Dr. Patricia Norris of the Karl Menninger Foundation, who teaches patients to use mind power to combat disease, tells the story of a nine-year-old boy who cured himself of a malignant tumor using a "*Star Wars*" visualization technique:

> "Garret Potter was a terminal case—it was estimated he had only about six months to live. He had a virulent, malignant type of tumor. Radiation treatments had failed. Surgery was out of the question because of the tumor's location. If he fell down he couldn't pick himself up.
>
> "Using his mind he visualized his immune system as powerful. It was a *Star Wars*-like visualization—he saw his brain as the solar system and his tumor as an evil invading villain. He visualized himself as the leader of a space fighter squadron fighting the tumor and winning.

"Garret used the technique for twenty minutes each night. At first his condition worsened and then it gradually began to get better. Five months later a brain scan was taken. The tumor was gone.

"The visualization technique was the only therapy employed after it had been concluded that the radiation therapy had failed."

Everyone is different. The technique which worked for Garret Potter may not be appropriate for everyone. Sometimes a gentler approach is needed.

Dr. David Bresler, director of the Los Angeles Pain Control Unit, describes a technique he used to help a patient. "The guy was in terrible pain. We'd tried everything we could think of. Finally I decided to use guided imagery." Telling the man to take a comfortable position in an office chair, Dr. Bresler asked him to picture his pain as concretely as possible. The patient soon said that he could "see" a large vicious dog snapping at his spine. He was then asked to imagine himself making friends with the dog, talking to it. As he did so, the patient found his pain subsiding until, after a few sessions, it disappeared. Like many people he recovered his health only when he stopped fighting his illness.

Athlete Kevin O'Neal saved his career by using the power of his mind. After a serious cycling accident, one of his hands was badly shattered and his confidence shaken just weeks before a major triathalon, but he visualized going inside his body and physically putting his broken bones together. As a result of his visualization, the bones healed twice as fast as expected and he was able to compete in the event.

The stories go on and on.

Dr. Paul Rennie of Vancouver, British Columbia sums it up nicely when he says, "The mind is one untapped resource we have yet to fully explore. This is what we should be investigating." And no less an authority than Nobel laureate Joshua Lederberg has called this area of investigation "the most important step in medicine today."

Our health is our responsibility. We must take an active role in our health and healing. If sick, we should not just give way to our illness but should share in the responsibility for our treatment. When all is said and done, as Dr. Albert Schweitzer always proclaimed, "the real doctor is the doctor within."

SEVENTEEN

Prosperity Consciousness

*To you the Earth yields her fruit,
and you shall not want if you
know how to fill your hands.*
—Kahlil Gibran

Anyone desiring financial independence must first develop a "prosperity consciousness." Notice I said "develop" because prosperity consciousness does not happen by chance. No one is born with it, nor can it be given to you. It is a state of mind tuned and vibrating to expect, acknowledge, and see prosperity and opportunities everywhere.

The opposite of prosperity consciousness is "scarcity consciousness," and it's all most people know. Scarcity consciousness expects and acknowledges lack and limitation and sees it everywhere, like signposts on a road which seems to lead only to want, poverty and hard times. No one will ever achieve financial success with a scarcity consciousness. It isn't possible.

You cannot simultaneously travel both the path to riches and the path to poverty, for they go in opposite directions. Both roads are clearly marked; there is no great mystery—whatever path you have chosen to travel will determine what will ultimately happen to you.

Do you have prosperity consciousness or scarcity consciousness? If you find you have scarcity consciousness, your task is clear. You must rid yourself of this mental ball and chain and develop the necessary prosperity consciousness.

There are five steps to follow in building a prosperity consciousness:

STEP 1: DEVELOP PROSPERITY BELIEFS

There are *four* main prosperity beliefs.

Prosperity Belief #1

It's an abundant universe.
Prosperity consciousness believes it's an abundant universe, that there is lots of everything for everyone if we but open ourselves up to it. Look at nature—lavish, extravagant, even wasteful in its abundance. Try and count the number of stars in the sky: you cannot, no one ever has or ever will; they number in the hundreds of billions. Look at wildflowers in a field spreading out far beyond what your eyes can see. Everywhere you look there is abundance. Likewise, in the marketplace opportunities exist everywhere if you focus your mind to see them. The only scarcity that exists is in our own consciousness.

Scarcity consciousness says, "There's not enough to go around," "If I have a lot then someone else goes without," or, "If I get a promotion someone else misses out."

Scarcity consciousness believes that "everyone is competing against everyone else for the same things" and that "there are no opportunities," or that "there's very little money" and "everything is so expensive." Watch closely to see if you have any of these beliefs, for it is a sure sign that scarcity consciousness has crept into your mind.

Prosperity Belief #2:

Life is fun and rewarding.
Scarcity consciousness believes that life is hard and filled with problems and difficulties. Scarcity consciousness believes you have to work hard for everything you get.

I've met many people who believe "you have to work hard for everything you get" and they always work hard for everything. How could it be otherwise with that belief? Remember what I said earlier about beliefs? The conscious mind will always give you ample evidence to support whatever belief you choose. Many people believe that life is harsh and difficult and, for them, it always is. Scarcity consciousness looks for and expects problems, difficulties, disappointments and frustrations, and it always finds them.

Prosperity consciousness looks at life as an adventure. It expects rewards. It looks for the fun and joy in life and always finds them. When problems and difficulties come they are seen as challenges, and the opportunities that each contains are sought after and used. Prosperity consciousness appreciates life and knows that with every new challenge comes greater rewards, new adventures, more fun. Life is full, rich and rewarding, and new experiences and more success lie just around every corner.

Prosperity Belief #3:

There are staggering numbers of opportunities in every aspect of my life.
Scarcity consciousness believes there are no opportunities

around, that the best you can expect is what is happening right now. It tricks you into believing that it doesn't matter what you do, that all the good ideas have been taken or that the time isn't right to start new ones. With scarcity consciousness the situation is always hopeless and there's never any point in trying.

Prosperity consciousness believes there are staggering numbers of opportunities in every aspect of your life, staggering numbers! Not one or two or five or ten, but staggering numbers of opportunities. "Where are they?" you ask. Why, everywhere! Open up your eyes, *open up your mind* with prosperity consciousness and you'll quickly begin to see them.

Let me share with you a story which illustrates this. Several years ago on Easter Sunday I got up early and hid ten small presents for the special woman in my life. The minute she awoke, I told her I had hidden some presents for her. She bounded from the bed, began searching excitedly, and after half an hour had found three presents. She sat down quite happily thinking that was all there were. "There's more than that," I said, which had her up in a flash searching for more. She managed to find two more and then, thinking there couldn't possibly be any more, she stopped looking. After lunch I casually mentioned, "Oh, by the way, I hid ten presents."

"Ten?" she exclaimed in amazement and again began searching, going over the same area but this time really looking hard. She eventually found all ten, but had I not told her there were ten presents she would have stopped at three, fully believing she'd found them all. Likewise, if you believe there are only a limited number of opportunities, then chances are that you will find only a few, if any. Why make any further effort searching for opportunities that don't exist?

But if you believe there are staggering numbers of opportunities in every aspect of your life, then you will actively search them out. Think about it!

Staggering opportunities for abundant health.
Staggering opportunities to make new relationships.
Staggering opportunities to advance yourself.
Staggering opportunities to become closer to your family.
Staggering opportunities to live a fun-filled life.
Staggering numbers of opportunities to make a great deal of money.

Let's look at making money.

I love the free enterprise system. I love a system that rewards ingenuity and imagination. Anyone can make a great deal of money if armed with the right ideas and the right attitude. The marketplace is an exciting phenomenon, dynamic and ever-changing, seething with opportunities waiting to be tried. Tens of billions of dollars exchange hands every day. Money is in constant motion, flowing in every direction, so why not take your share by contributing to the system?

Each year in North America over 700,000 new businesses open. Every single one of them represents new opportunities, for each will need printing, accounting, legal work, advertising, staff, maintenance, signs, office furniture. Opportunities, opportunities everywhere.

The United States, in 1940, had 10,000 millionaires. In 1980 the population doubled, but the number of millionaires had mushroomed to 500,000. By 1997, this number had swelled to over two million. Even considering inflation, this is an astonishing increase. Opportunities, opportunities everywhere.

Never before in the history of civilization has there been an environment as rapidly changing as the one we live in today. Things are changing all the time, and what is new and revolutionary this week becomes outdated in six months. This whirlwind environment means that opportunities are rapidly being created each and every hour. Every day there are thousands of new opportunities that didn't exist yesterday. Opportunities, opportunities everywhere.

Billionaire Bill Gates, co-founder of Microsoft, shares these sentiments: "I think this is a wonderful time to be alive. There have never been so many opportunities to do things that were impossible before. It's the best time ever to start new companies and ventures."

Where are your opportunities? Jump into the action and find them; they surround you.

Prosperity Belief #4:

It is my responsibility to be successful.
Scarcity consciousness believes that having lots of money is wrong, that you should only have enough for your basic needs, and that having anything beyond that deprives other people. Scarcity consciousness believes that successful people are selfish, greedy, neglect their families and have their priorities wrong.

Prosperity consciousness believes that having lots of money is good and that it is your responsibility to be successful. It believes this because it understands that the more money you make, the greater your potential for helping people, especially financially. It only makes sense: how can a philanthropist give a charity ten or ten thousand dollars if he hasn't allowed himself to acquire it in the first place? Money can be used in many ways to help and benefit those around us. Enjoy your prosperity and help others to prosper as well. When you are prosperous you can give to many charities, help friends, give to those less fortunate, create an immense amount of financial energy and direct it wherever you wish. It is your duty and responsibility to become successful, have lots of money, and help all those you can to prosper in their lives as well.

The first step in building a prosperity consciousness is to imprint the four prosperity beliefs into your subconscious mind.

1. *It's an abundant universe.*
2. *Life is fun and rewarding.*
3. *Staggering opportunities exist for me in every aspect of my life.*
4. *It is my responsibility to be successful.*

STEP 2: LOOK FOR AND ACKNOWLEDGE
ABUNDANCE IN THE NOW OF YOUR LIFE

You are surrounded by abundance right now; all you need to do is open your eyes and look for it. Don't wait for money to come your way before you feel prosperous. Feel prosperous now! Do you have an abundance of friends? An abundance of good health? An abundance of ideas or clothes or time? Look for areas of your life where you can feel the abundance.

HOW I PROGRAMMED MY MIND
FOR PROSPERITY AND BECAME WEALTHY

Let me tell you how I first began programming my mind for prosperity. I was living in a small cabin deep in the woods with no electricity and no running water. I had no money, but I understood the principles of prosperity and began reprogramming my mind.

As I cut my firewood I would give thanks for the abundance all around me. While stacking the wood I would say, "Not one piece of wood, not two, not ten, but an abundance of wood to keep me warm." When I ate my meals I would praise myself and the universe for the abundance I had. If I had a bowl of grapes in front of me I would count them one by one: not just one grape, not just two grapes, but an abundance of grapes. Walking in the woods I would see prosperity all around me: fields filled with thousands of wild flowers, trees everywhere, birds and wildlife in abundance. Nature was indeed bountiful. Even though I had no money I kept my mind focused on abundance. I knew that if I kept my mind focused in this way, the manifestation of abundance would soon follow.

When I gave my first public lecture, because I had very little money I was staying in a third-class hotel. I was embarrassed about this and made sure no one saw me leave or enter. Often in the afternoons I would go into the lobby of a first-class hotel to absorb the energy and vibration of the place. Soon I was making enough money to stay in first-class hotels and I praised the universe for its abundance.

One day, while walking down the corridor of my hotel, I glanced into a room which was being cleaned and was amazed to see a large living room with no beds. I coaxed the cleaning woman to let me come in and look around, and I was surprised to see that there were two rooms—a large living room and a separate bedroom. It was my first introduction to a suite. That day I began visualizing myself staying in suites, and one day I finally rented one. I couldn't really afford it, but I wanted the vibration of wealth even if only for one evening. I walked around my suite feeling abundant. I sat down on the plush sofa and put my feet up on the table. This was real; I had made it to a suite even if it was just for one night. I praised the universe for its abundance. Gradually I began staying in suites more and more. At first I was making a little bit of money, then more, until lots of money was flowing my way.

Napoleon Hill, financial mentor to many great men, once exclaimed, "When big money begins to come it comes so quickly and in such large amounts, you wonder where it was hiding during all those lean years." It certainly worked that way with me. I still remember the day I realized I had really "arrived" financially.

It was at a party I was giving to celebrate my five-year anniversary of teaching "Thought Dynamics." I was in Sydney, Australia, on a world tour, and I was staying in the presidential suite at the Sheraton Hotel. It was a lavish suite—the living room was almost the size of the lobby. A huge glass wall ran from floor to ceiling across the entire suite and below me all Sydney lay at my feet: the opera house, the harbor, the sparkling city lights. It was a majestic sight.

I was entertaining my guests when I remember thinking, "What a change of fortune." I excused myself for a moment and went to the bedroom and then out onto the private balcony overlooking the ocean. In just five years I had gone from living in a cabin with no electricity or running water to entertaining my friends in the presidential suite of one of the world's finest hotels. Not only that, but I had checked in for an entire month—money was no longer an object. I thought back to how I first began programming my mind for prosperity, and the fruit that it now bore, and I thanked the universe for the secrets of success that had been revealed to me. I made a silent promise that I would pass these secrets on to others, and then I rejoined my guests.

Begin programming your mind *right now* for prosperity. I began my prosperity programming in deepest poverty.

There is no situation in which you can't begin prosperity programming.

STEP 3: RECOGNIZE AND ASSOCIATE WITH SUCCESS EVERYWHERE

Train yourself to see success everywhere you look.

Everywhere you look there is prosperity.

Go to the center of your city and look at the huge office towers. Think of all the success that is contained in just one of the buildings. You can be assured that the architect who designed the building made a great deal of money for doing so. The contractor who built the building probably made a small fortune. The owners of the building are obviously rich and successful men. The people who rent the lavish offices must also be successful. Now imagine how wealthy and powerful those who rent the top penthouse suites must be. Just that one building represents so much success, and you can multiply that success by the number of buildings in your city. And that's just the beginning. Prosperity consciousness recognizes that there is success all around us if we just open our eyes to see it.

Never begrudge someone else's good fortune. Acknowledge it and feel good about it, for it is proof that it can be done. Then confidently remind yourself that you can do it too. Look for and acknowledge success everywhere you can find it. It is scarcity consciousness which resents success and tries to put down those who've achieved it. Guard yourself against these thoughts as if they were a deadly poison for they are, indeed, mental poison to your personal prosperity.

Always acknowledge and feel joy and happiness every time you see success, whether it is your own or others. Open up your eyes and notice that success is everywhere, all around you, in abundance. It will be yours, too, if you can adjust your thinking to prosperity.

STEP 4: READ INSPIRATIONAL BOOKS, LISTEN TO SELF-HELP TAPES, JOIN GROUPS AND ORGANIZATIONS THAT DESIRE SUCCESS

Everything you do becomes a part of you. This book you are now reading is filled with life-changing principles that will make a tremendous impact on your life if you apply them. If you have the opportunity to attend my "Thought Dynamics" course, I encourage you to do so, but drink from all sources—self-help books and groups, literature, sound advice—anything that inspires you to succeed.

STEP 5: ASSOCIATE WITH SUCCESSFUL PEOPLE BOTH REAL AND IMAGINARY

If you want to be a filmmaker, associate with other film-makers.

If you want to be an artist, find other artists.

If you want to be successful, seek out the company of successful people.

The energy of success rubs off when you are in its company. Successful people think successful thoughts, make successful decisions, create successful plans, complete successful projects. You can pick up that energy and use it just by being in their company.

YOUR RESPONSIBILITY IS TO SUCCEED

You have to understand deeply that having what you want in life contributes to the general state of human happiness and supports others in creating success for themselves. Success never takes away from others, but rather, creates success for and helps others. The more successful an economy, the more opportunities exist for everyone. The more money you have, the more you spend on goods and services, which creates additional money and profit for other people to spend on goods and services, and so on.

When successful people help others it is an example to everyone, and so their success rubs off on everyone. You have a duty and responsibility to become successful for yourself, your children, your friends, and everyone who comes in contact with you. Everyone will benefit.

YOUR SUCCESS HELPS MANY PEOPLE
YOUR FAILURE HELPS NO ONE

Think about the above statement before you settle for anything less than success. Realize your success is more than just personal ambition; it is your responsibility. Don't be selfish, succeed. The world needs you!

EIGHTEEN

Fulfilling Relationships

I will act as if what I do makes a difference.

—William James

Personal relationships are as vital to us as the air we breathe. We all need friends, lovers, companions, people with whom we can share our joys, sorrows, fears and successes. These interactions touch and nourish us at our deepest levels. We all need friendship, love, caring companionship, and a feeling of belonging, and yet often we remain distant and detached from one another, unable or unwilling to reach out and make meaningful contact.

We need new approaches and a greater willingness to explore the possibilities that exist in human interaction. If we choose, we can be a great source of growth and support for each other and strengthen ourselves in the process. Discovering how we can enrich and empower one another is an exciting turning point in our journey toward more meaningful relationships. We find that when we open up, people respond and accept us for what we are. Instead of feeling vulnerable we become free, alive, vibrant and awakened in ways we never experienced before. When this happens, every contact becomes meaningful, important and enriching. What more could we ask?

EVERY PERSON IS A STAR

Every person is special, unique, and deserves respect. *Every* person is a star. Your husband. Your wife. Your parents, too, are special, unique and deserve respect. Every one of your friends, your boss, your waitress, a taxi driver, a dying old man, the neighbor's boy—all are special, unique and deserve your respect.

The realization that every person, no matter who they are or what their status, is special changes our attitude towards them. We now willingly grant them the respect they deserve. They may not know they are special or show it in their actions, but we know it, and treat them accordingly.

Learn to see beyond what people see in themselves. Everyone has the seed of greatness inside them and you empower people by seeing beyond their imperfections and problems to their potential, their depth, their inner beauty and their possibilities.

I first discovered the transforming power of treating every person as a star while lecturing in San Francisco some years ago. I was traveling with an associate and his family. We had difficulty in finding a baby-sitter and had to settle for a woman who was one of the most negative and draining persons I had ever met. She complained constantly about anything and everything, and whenever she arrived we tried to leave immediately so as not to have to spend too much time with her. I found myself thinking quite negatively about her and, catching myself, I decided to make some changes in my thoughts. I realized that deep down there was someone else inside, someone deeper and more joyous than the one we were seeing. I concentrated on picturing her in this way until I laughingly began thinking of her as the "ray of sunshine."

The next time she came over, instead of rushing out of the house I took her aside and said, "You know, every time you come into this house, it's like a ray of sunshine coming in." She looked at me dumbfounded. I went on, "We really appreciate you and your being our baby-sitter, and we're happy that we have someone like you here." She was speechless. When we returned home later that evening, I again began praising her as "a ray of sunshine."

The next time she came over I greeted her with, "Look! The ray of sunshine is here," and I meant it, for deep down I knew there was someone beautiful and wonderful there.

She smiled at me—the first time I had ever seen her smile. When the others left the room she said to me, "You know something? Nobody has ever said something nice like that to me before. Never. Not in my whole life." I was stunned. Shocked. I couldn't imagine someone never once having something nice said to them. I wondered about her childhood and what misfortunes she had suffered throughout her life; what a hard life she must have had. I was glad I had changed my thoughts toward her, and ashamed at how I had previously put her down.

I continued to feed her positive, supportive energy and the result was startling. She stopped complaining, became pleasant, and—amazingly—within weeks the lines on her face disappeared and she looked twenty years younger. Everyone noticed it. She actually became "a ray of sunshine." This incident forever changed the way I look at people.

When you recognize people as worthy of respect, they tend to respond accordingly. You empower people by seeing the greatness in them. Maybe people don't see themselves as great and unique. Perhaps they feel worthless. Well, be their mirror! Show them that you see their potential. Show them with your acts, words, thoughts and feelings. Every person's life is important. Every person has a contribution to make. Treat each of them as special. Your support could well be the boost or turning point in someone's life, so don't let a person's outward appearance blind you to their greatness. Bring out the best in everyone by believing in them.

As you adopt this attitude toward people you will develop meaningful relationships with everyone you meet, and even a casual exchange will enrich both you and the other person. Our ability to help, love and share with one another is immense; all we need is the desire to do so.

HUMAN: HANDLE WITH CARE

We human beings are sensitive creatures. If you doubt this, look at yourself and see how easily you can be hurt or become offended. When wounded themselves, people hurt others. I discovered this by looking closely at myself. Whenever I was mean or hurtful toward someone else, it was always because I was suffering deep down myself.

Remember this the next time someone does something unpleasant to you. Ask yourself what pain might be inside them, and feel love and compassion for them. It's no fun for them to be aching inside. We don't know what fears, scars, disappointments, insecurities and difficulties people carry within them. As the old saying goes, "Don't judge a person till you've walked a mile in his shoes."

A woman who was taking my "Thought Dynamics" course

was thinking of leaving her job because a co-worker was so thoroughly obnoxious. My student had built up a strong dislike for this woman; in fact the two were not even speaking to one another. Things had been like this for almost a year when she decided to try something different.

Realizing that perhaps her co-worker was unpleasant because of some deep inner hurt, my student began thinking kinder thoughts toward her, and no longer let herself harbor her old resentments. Every time her co-worker was unpleasant she silently sent love to her. No longer did she react and get upset, but began actively empowering the woman, remembering that deep down the woman was special, unique and deserved respect. She began a nightly program of visualizing the woman as being pleasant, warm and loving; she knew that, at her core, the woman was like that. She visualized herself and her co-worker as friends. Finally, one day she went over to the woman, apologized for not talking, and said she wanted to be friends. The woman was startled and didn't respond, but within days her mood changed. Now the two are friends and their working atmosphere is joyful and pleasant.

This happens all the time. I can't count the number of times I have heard similar stories from people who changed a relationship by changing the thoughts and attitudes they held toward the other person.

AS YOU CHANGE YOUR THOUGHTS TOWARD PEOPLE, PEOPLE CHANGE TOWARD YOU

Because human beings are so sensitive to each other on so many levels, we are extremely receptive to the thought forms we hold about each other. If your relationship with your lover, friend, business partner, fellow-worker or parent is not what you want it to be, look closely at what thought forms you are unconsciously creating about that person. You may be clinging to and reinforcing the very qualities you dislike in them.

In relationships, as in everything else, we get exactly what we believe in, think of, and expect to happen. There are many possibilities in every relationship if you are willing to experiment with your thoughts. Visualization allows you to build new thought forms and become a creator in your relationships. Create, don't react.

ATTRACT THE RELATIONSHIPS YOU DESIRE

How to attract the ideal mate:

Step 1: Picture in your mind the type of person you want. What qualities are you looking for? Do you have a physical ideal? Visualize yourself with someone like that, experiencing tender moments, sharing intimacy, laughing, having fun, going on outings. Create your ideal companion in the inner world of your thoughts. Don't try and put a face on this person or be *too* specific; let the universe supply it to you within the specifications you mentally imagine.

Step 2: Focus on what you can give to this person. You have lots to offer. Feel good about yourself and think of all you have to give and share with that person.

Step 3: Solicit the help of your unseen partner—your subconscious mind. Ask your subconscious to supply you with the ways and means to meet this special person. Reread the chapter on intuition and follow the instructions and ideas your subconscious supplies you with.

Step 4: Contemplate these points: There are thousands of people who would love to be with you to share what you have to give. Your visualizations, affirmations and intuitions are setting in motion forces which will bring you into contact with your ideal mate. Remember that that person is looking for someone like you, too.

How to attract business contacts:

Step 1: Picture in your mind the type of person you want to work with, and what contacts, skills, information or knowledge you would like them to have. If you need a pearl diver fluent in Japanese, picture that. If you are trying to get a job as a freelance journalist, picture an editor with an assignment in your area of expertise or in an area that interests you. Visualize yourself with that person enjoying good rapport, a firm connection and mutual receptivity to one another's proposals.

Step 2: Focus on what you can give to this person, what talents, products or expertise you can supply. Not only do you need them, but they need you and what you can offer.

Step 3: Solicit the help of your unseen partner—your subconscious mind. Ask it to supply you with the ways and means of meeting this person. Reread the chapter on intuition and follow the instructions and ideas your subconscious supplies.

Step 4: Contemplate these points: There are thousands of business opportunities and people who would love to have what you can offer. Your visualizations, affirmations and intuition set in motion energy and forces which will bring you into contact with these people.

Do you want to attract more clients or customers? Do the above exercises focusing on what kind of clients you want and what you have to give them. A good affirmation in both cases is, "I attract the perfect people and circumstances."

EMPOWERING OTHERS

We can empower other people with a minimum amount of effort on our part. In doing so, we strengthen both ourselves and the other person. Empowering people is a special and intimate way of touching others' lives.

Once, while waiting at New York's J.F.K. Airport, an announcement came over the P.A. system that my flight was canceled and that passengers should proceed to "Counter 7" for further instructions.

When I arrived at Counter 7, there was already a sizeable line-up and, as I waited my turn, I noticed almost everyone was venting their frustration on the harried ticket agent. People were anxious and furious about their missed connections and were asking, "What are we supposed to do?" The ticket agent looked tired and drawn as she tried to explain the situation, and her shoulders seemed to slump lower and lower with each new passenger complaint. When my turn came I decided to empower her. "I really appreciate all you are doing," I remarked sincerely. "I know this is a difficult situation and I know you're doing your very best. I've noticed how courteous and patient you've been with people and I know it's not your fault the flight is canceled." She sighed in relief that someone understood. I went on, "I just want to thank you and tell you I think you're doing a terrific job and that you should be proud of yourself."

"Thanks," she said, "I really needed that."

After receiving her instructions I moved on, but happened to look back at her as she faced the next passenger. She was standing upright again looking poised and confident. I had given her some needed energy. How simple and easy it was for me to express my appreciation, yet it made a real difference to her.

Can you empower people just by what you say? Of course! You can empower everyone you meet if you want to do so. You can empower the waitress after a meal, the delivery person, the taxi driver, the letter carrier, your children and your friends by feeding them positive energy.

"We really appreciate the fine service you are giving us. You are making our meal a joy and a pleasure. You're a very good waiter."

"You are my favorite teller. I'm always pleased when you serve me. How has your day been?"

"Thank you very much!"

"That's an extremely attractive outfit you're wearing."

Even a simple, "Have a good day!" if said with sincerity, enthusiasm and a genuine desire to make contact, will empower anyone.

You can also empower people without saying anything, just by using your thoughts. A friend of mine likes to walk down the street silently sending out thoughts of goodwill to everyone he passes. A successful businessman I know silently affirms with everyone he meets that they will have a happy and successful life.

Thoughts of love and acceptance free people. Kind words and encouragement inspire them. Acknowledging people strengthens them. Making people feel special, wanted and needed empowers them. That simple effort can have results that can last for days, or even a lifetime.

EMPOWERING OURSELVES

Sometimes we forget that the most intimate and closest relationship we will ever experience is with our own self. Be good to yourself; don't be too hard on yourself. Remember that you, too, are special, unique and deserve respect.

We are told to "love thy neighbor as thyself," and the emphasis is always on "love thy neighbor." But if we are to love our neighbor we must first learn to love ourselves. And if we want to love our neighbor more, then we must learn to love ourselves more. The more deeply we love and accept ourselves, the deeper we can love and accept others.

Empower yourself so you can become strong, loving and healthy. *Acknowledge* your own uniqueness often and regularly. *Affirm* good things about and for yourself. Visualize yourself as successful, loving, open and free. *Work* on your self-image and make it strong and confident. Like yourself. Love yourself. Be a good friend to yourself.

NURTURING OUR RELATIONSHIPS

When was the last time you told a friend you loved them? When was the last time you thanked someone for their support, friendship or love? Deepen your relationships by appreciating others and sharing that appreciation. "I really value and treasure our friendship," when said with feeling, can mean so much.

There are no greater riches in the world than friendship and human contact. Be a good friend to everyone you meet. Be there for other people. Accept people. Love people. Love unconditionally, whether or not they like or respond to you. Don't wait for others to make the first move. Open up. What have you got to lose except your isolation?

TRANSFORMING RELATIONSHIPS
MEANS TRANSFORMING OURSELVES

We are all members of the same universal family and, as such, must make ourselves available to one another in more loving, caring and fulfilling ways if we wish to grow. The road to fulfilling relationships is a journey of change and growth. It means risking, exploring and even stumbling sometimes. It starts with little things: a changed attitude, a reaching out, a look exchanged on a bus, a moment of total honesty with a stranger, but it soon grows into something much larger and more rewarding. It becomes a celebration, a joyful way of living in which we are open and aware in ways we never experienced before.

NINETEEN

Training for the Magnificent Pay-off

We all love to win, but how many people love to train?

—Mark Spitz

I t was 1972 in Munich. A relatively unknown swimmer was poised at the edge of the pool awaiting the firing of the starter gun. It was his first time in the Olympics and he had made it to the finals. The gun sounded and he dove into the pool and swam with all his strength. Moments later he had won the gold medal and set a new world record at the same time. The next day he swam again, and again won another gold medal and, amazingly, he again won it in world record time. He swam seven races in Munich, won seven gold medals and, incredibly, established seven new world records. It was one of the greatest feats in Olympic history. The entire world suddenly knew the name of Mark Spitz.

But behind this glory was a dedication to training that had seen Mark swimming and lifting weights hour after hour, day after day, year after year, in preparation for the 1972 Olympics. His winning was not luck or chance but the end result of all the work he had put into his sport. He had the heart of a champion, and the dedication of one who knows what he wants and what he has to do to achieve it. His words call for careful attention from all who wish to excel: "We all love to win," he said, "but how many people love to train?"

To use mind power effectively does not, thankfully, take the dedication of an Olympic champion. If it did, few of us would be able to use it. But there is a commitment of time required. It doesn't just happen magically.

Reading this book is only the first formative step in developing and using mind power. No one truly understands the system or its benefits until they have practiced it for at least thirty days, and the real benefits emerge only after sixty to ninety days. Often noticeable changes do happen within the first few days or weeks, but these are not to be confused with the lasting results that come with continued practice.

Above all, let the student remember that for steady growth, regular practice is essential. When a day's practice is omitted, three or four days' work are necessary to counterbalance the slipping back, at least during the earlier stages of growth. Better five minutes of work done regularly than half an hour on some days and none on others.

THE VISION

Nobody works without the thought of compensation. The Olympic athlete trains long and hard because the goal of a gold medal and the satisfaction of being the world's best lie before her.

A laborer goes to work each day because a pay check awaits him at the end of each week.

An entrepreneur devotes her entire attention to her business because she reaps the fruits of her success.

A handyman spends his evenings fixing up the basement because he knows his efforts will eventually result in a cozy recreation room.

Behind all effort is the thought of the pay-off, the fruits of the labor. If there is no compensation, then there is no reason or motivation to work; few of us work for the sheer love of it.

The 21st century will require new skills. Intuition, dream interpretation, visualization and creativity are just some of the tools we will need to be successful. You are standing on the threshold of a new and exciting age. This book contains the methods by which you can learn the necessary skills and thereby harness your mind for maximum potential. But it takes more than just reading this book. You must train your mind.

Do you have the vision of what training mentally will do for you?

If you think of mind power as "positive thinking" or "an interesting concept," or think, "maybe it will work, and maybe it won't," then you will never make the effort necessary to train your mind. It is only the grand vision of what we can do and become that propels us to work regularly at creating our new reality.

There is a glorious life of power and opportunity awaiting you. Everything that you can conceive of wanting is within your grasp. The time is ripe and ready. Are you?

Reread this book carefully, studying all the principles. Train regularly and soon you will receive *The Magnificent Pay-off*.

Visit with John at Home

As a writer committed to staying in touch with his readers, John Kehoe personally invites you to join him via the Internet to share your Mind Power questions and observations. Each month, from his home, John will respond to a selection of correspondence on matters of interest to his ever-expanding community of readers and students. You'll also find this exciting new site loaded with important news and information updates, tour schedules, interesting links, and tips on using Mind Power to get the most out of life! Contact John by directing your browser to:

http://www.kehoe-mindpower.com

Suggested Readings

Twenty-five years of research and twenty years of teaching have gone into this book. Having a naturally inquisitive mind and being a voracious reader I actively sought out any material related to human potential and to the human mind in particular. This inquiry has led me down many interesting labyrinths, some of which have proved very fruitful and others which have not been so valuable. My own personal growth (yes, I do practice what I preach) and the insights I've received by training and teaching others in workshops around the world have given me a good understanding of the human mind and the incredible powers it possesses.

Rather than list every book and source I have consulted (many of which I can no longer remember), I'd prefer to share with you the ones I found especially valuable. This way the ardent student can pursue further studies according to his or her own inclination. The following, in no particular order, are books and sources I can recommend.

The Tao of Physics, Fritjof Capra
The Aquarian Conspiracy, Marilyn Ferguson
The Power of Your Subconscious Mind, Joseph Murphy
In Tune with the Infinite, Ralph Waldo Trine
The Nature of Personal Reality, Jane Roberts
Jungian Dream Interpretation, James Hall

The Way of the Dream, Fraser Boa
The Little Course in Dreams, Robert Bosnak
The Mystical Qabalah, Dion Fortune
The Zen Environment, Marian Mountain
The Three Pillars of Zen, Roshi Philip Kapleau
Seeker of Visions, Lame Deer
The Edgar Cayce Handbook for Creating your Future,
    Mark Thruston and Christopher Fazel
Super Learning, Sheila Ostrander and Lynn Schroeder
Think and Grow Rich, Napoleon Hill
The Master Key, Charles Haamel Schroeder
The Magical Child, Joseph Pearce
Apprenticed to Magic, W.E. Butler
A Course in Miracles: Foundation for Inner Peace
Quantum Consciousness, Stephen Wolinsky
The Holographic Universe, Michael Talbot
The Complete Works of Carl Jung, Joseph Campbell and
    Jean Houston

Visit our web site at http://www.kehoe-mindpower.com